WITHDRAWN

363.1241
S532ai

P9-APT-529

AIR
DISASTERS

Brown
PARTWORKS

AIR
DISASTERS

MIKE SHARPE

Copyright © 1998 Brown Partworks Limited

This edition published in 1999 by Brown Partworks,
8 Chapel Place, Rivington St, London EC2A 3DQ, England.

All rights reserved. No part of this publication may be
reproduced, stored in a retrieval system, or transmitted,
in any form or by any means without the prior written
permission of the publisher, nor to be otherwise circulated
in any form of binding or cover other than that in which
it is published and without a similar condition being
imposed on the subsequent purchaser.

ISBN 1-84044-026-0

Printed and bound in Dubai

For Brown Partworks Ltd

Editor: Shona Grimbly
Design: Wilson Design Associates
Picture research: Wendy Verren
Production: Alex MacKenzie

Photographic credits:
Cover, tl, Rex Features; c and tr, Popperfoto;
1, Getty Images; 2-3, Rex Features; 5, Popperfoto; 6, Corbis-Bettmann/UPI;
7t, Popperfoto/Reuters; 7b, Popperfoto/Duncan Pettenden/Reuters; 8, Corbis-Bettmann/
UPI; 9t, Popperfoto/AFP; 9b, Getty Images; 11, Popperfoto/Antony Njuguna/Reuters;
12, Hugh W Cowin; 13, Hugh W Cowin; 14, Hugh W Cowin; 15, Hugh W Cowin;
16t, Popperfoto, 16b, Popperfoto; 17, TRH/J Widdowson; 18, TRH/Boeing; 19t, Popperfoto;
19b, Popperfoto; 20, Hugh W Cowin; 21t, TRH Pictures; 21b, TRH/DOD/Hughes; 22, Rex
Features; 23t, Popperfoto; 23b, Rex Features; 24, Popperfoto; 25, Popperfoto;
26t, Popperfoto; 26c, Popperfoto; 26b, Popperfoto; 27, Popperfoto/AFP; 29, Popperfoto;
30, Popperfoto; 31t, Getty Images; 31b, Corbis-Bettmann/UPI; 32, Getty Images;
33, Getty Images; 34, Getty Images; 35, Jose F. Poblete/Corbis; 36t, Associated Press;
36b, Associated Press; 37, Tony Stone Images; 38, Corbis-Bettmann/UPI, 39, TRH Pictures;
40, Popperfoto; 41, Hugh W Cowin; 42, Corbis-Bettmann/UPI; 43, Popperfoto, 45, Popperfoto;
46, Corbis Bettmann/Ryall; 47t, TRH/Rockwell Int.; 47b, Popperfoto; 48, David Muench/
Corbis; 49t, Associated Press; 49b, Associated Press; 50, Popperfoto; 51t, Popperfoto;
51b, Popperfoto; 52, TRH/Boeing; 53, Rex Features; 54t, Rex Features; 54b, Corbis-
Bettmann/UPI; 55, Popperfoto; 56, Rex Features/Sipa Press; 57, Popperfoto; 58t, Popperfoto;
58b, Popperfoto; 59, Popperfoto; 61, Rex Features/Sipa Press; 62, Popperfoto;
63t, Popperfoto; 63b, Getty Images; 64, TRH Pictures; 65t, TRH/USN; 65b, Popperfoto;
66, TRH Pictures; 67t, Popperfoto; 67b, Popperfoto; 68, Robert Hunt Picture Library;
69, Corbis-Bettmann/UPI; 70, Corbis-Bettmann/UPI; 71, TRH/E Nevill; 72t, Corbis-
Bettmann/UPI; 72b, Corbis-Bettmann/UPI; 73, Rex Features/Sipa Press; 75, Rex Features;
76, TRH Pictures; 77t, TRH Pictures; 77b, TRH Pictures; 77b, Popperfoto; 78, Getty
Images; 79, TRH Pictures; 80, Popperfoto; 81, Getty Images; 82t, Getty Images; 82b, Corbis-
Bettmann/UPI; 83, Corbis-Bettmann/UPI; 84t, Corbis-Bettmann/UPI; 84b, Corbis-Bettmann/
UPI; 85, Popperfoto; 86; Popperfoto; 87t, Getty Images; 87b, Popperfoto; 88, Popperfoto;
89, Popperfoto; 90, Popperfoto; 91, Hugh W Cowin; 92, Corbis-Bettmann/Reuters; 93, Rex
Features; 94t, TRH Pictures; 94b, Popperfoto; 95, Popperfoto.

While every effort has been made to trace the copyright of the photographs and
illustrations used in this publication, there may be an instance where an error has
been made in the picture credits. If this is the case, we apologize for the mistake
and ask the copyright holder to contact the publisher so that it can be rectified.

Page 1: *The wreckage of the BOAC Boeing 707 airliner that crashed into Mount Fuji, Japan, on March 5, 1966 killing all 124 people on board.*

Pages 2-3: *US Coast Guards amd FBI investigators watch as a tangled piece of the wreckage of the TWA Boeing 747 is raised from the waters off Long Island, New York. The 747 exploded in mid air killing all on booard.*

Below right: *The scene just outside the Welsh village of Sigginston, where the Tudor V aircraft crashed on March 13, 1950 killing almost all the Welsh Rugby football supporters on board.*

CONTENTS

INTRODUCTION

This book sets out to provide an overview of some of the multiplicity of causes that have led to fatal air crashes since the beginnings of commercial aviation in the 1930s. The length or depth of each analysis is in no way a reflection of the relative impact of that accident – behind every fatal accident is a story of human tragedy.

The emphasis is on US/European accidents simply because these are the two areas where the vast majority of air traffic in the world originates.

The reader may disagree with the categories into which some of the disasters have been placed. Was the R101 airship, for example, downed by a violent storm or because it was inherently not airworthy? It might also be argued that a number of the entries in the chapter on air

and ground collision could just as easily have been attributed to human error.

Research for this book has only reinforced the belief that air travel is by far the safest form of transportation readily available to the world today. With three exceptions every accident analysed here involved a commercial transport aircraft, but in the 70-year period covered, these accidents are statistically insignificant when compared to the hundreds of millions of miles safely flown. In terms of the advances made in safety, air travel is simply leagues ahead of travel by road, rail, or ship. The improvements in aircraft technology that have made this so have not been matched in any other mode of transportation. Over long distances, air travel is also the most cost-effective, both for the regular business flier and the tourist.

Right: Rescuers searching the remains of the fuselage of the Turkish DC-10 that crashed in a forest near Senlis outside Paris on March 3, 1974

Inevitably, and thankfully rarely, things do go wrong. It is part of the very nature of air travel that when accidents do occur, the results are often catastrophic and involve heavy loss of life. However, it may come as a surprise to even the most seasoned traveler to be told that, on average, no more than 1500 people a year are killed in fatal air accidents.

As in many other areas of human progress, the pace of development in manned flight has proved costly in terms of human life. These deaths were of course tragic, but the lessons learned from the air disasters described in this book have helped to make air travel safer for everyone.

In the pioneering days of aviation however, the phrase "on a wing and a prayer" was more than apt. The risks of flying were at times considerable, but insufficient to deter that first generation of air travelers from the adventure that is still a very real part of flying for many people. Passengers are the life blood of an airline, and their confidence is a vital element in an airline's continued success.

This confidence has at times been compromised by people within the industry, whose negligence or misjudgments have led to tragedies that could have been avoided. Some of the disasters described in this book have forced air passengers to reevaluate their faith in the airline industry. Passenger safety should of course be the paramount concern of any commercial airline. Unfortunately it has to be said that this has sometimes taken second place to the financial pressures of a highly competitive business.

There are of course a number of factors beyond the control of air carriers. One of these is deliberate sabotage or aggression from an individual or group seeking financial or political gain from the destruction

Above: *An officer watches as Irish sailors and rescue workers carry ashore the body of one of the victims of the Air India crash in the Atlantic off the coast of Ireland on June 23, 1985.*

Right: *A diver searches the seabed for remains from the Ethiopian airliner that went down in the Indian ocean after being hijacked.*

of an aircraft. It may come as a surprise that the history of such incidents dates back to the 1930s, since most of the major hijacking incidents have taken place since the late 1960s. By singling out such a high profile target as a jet airliner an extremist group can gain worldwide media exposure that would otherwise be denied them. This was certainly the motive behind the actions of groups such as Black September, the Palestinian extremist group responsible for several atrocities.

Although less numerically significant, aggressive acts have been perpetrated by the defense forces of some countries – the US and the USSR among them –

against civilian aircraft. These events have occasionally resulted from an encroachment into the aggressor country's airspace, but whatever the motive such a wanton act of destruction is roundly condemned by the international aviation community. The designated airways that crisscross the world are heavily restricted by international political disputes, militarily-sensitive airspace, or because of dense urban areas. The price of a simple navigational error can be tragically high, as was demonstrated in September 1983 when a Korean airliner strayed into Soviet airspace and was shot down by the Soviet Air Force.

Below: An aerial view of the rescue vehicles and wreckage of the Eastern Airlines Boeing 727 that crashed at JFK airport, New York, on June 24, 1975.

Right: Rescue workers inspect the scene of destruction left when an El Al jumbo jet crashed into an apartment block in Amsterdam on October 4, 1992.

Below: Japanese rescue personnel search through the wreckage of the Boeing 707 that crashed into a forest at the foot of Mount Fuji on March 5, 1966.

Rigorous safety and pilot selection procedures, and the automation of many tasks performed by the pilot, are slowly removing the possibility of pilot error from passenger-carrying aircraft. Modern fly-by-wire control systems are programmed to analyse control inputs by the pilot and assess the possibility of the aircraft becoming unstable as a result. Pilot error has been a major factor in air disasters since the 1980s, but this will be reduced as procedures are further improved.

Adverse weather conditions have also contributed to a number of accidents that are included in a separate chapter in this book. Incidents of this type have been reduced drastically, predominantly because of advances in weather prediction technology, yet it has been said that mother nature can be a cruel mistress, and will continue to present a hazard to aircraft for the perceivable future.

Aircraft manufacturing techniques and materials have improved immeasurably since the early days of aviation, as have the tests that aircraft are subjected to before they are deemed fit to fly. There is no doubt that the second half of the 20th century saw a quantum leap in the safety of passenger aircraft. Much of this was due to the millions that aircraft manufacturers spent in looking for ways to further improve the safety of their products. Fortunately, this emphasis on safety, despite the tragic mishaps recorded in this book, is a common feature throughout the industry.

ACTS OF AGGRESSION

One of the most terrifying experiences the passengers and crew of an aircraft can undergo is to be hijacked by terrorists. Terrorism directed against aircraft has featured in the history of aviation since the 1930s. Hijackers and bombers can be either politically or financially motivated, or mentally unbalanced. For political extremists there is perhaps no better way of gaining international publicity, infamy, and ultimately notoriety than by hijacking an airliner.

There was a dramatic upsurge in the number of this type of incident during the late 1960s and early 1970s, most of them directly attributable to Arab terrorist organizations. However horrifying these incidents were, they had one good result. The vast improvements in airline security that followed them are rapidly consigning the hijacker to the history books.

Acts of aggression against civilian aircraft by military forces are rarely premeditated, but they are equally difficult to excuse since the lives of innocent people may be lost. In the 1980s both superpowers – the US and the USSR – received international condemnation for attacking passenger airliners that had been mistakenly identified as military aircraft. In one incident this almost certainly provoked an act of reprisal that cost more innocent people their lives.

Right: Police and military inspect the remains of the Ethiopian airliner that was hijacked on November 23, 1996, and subsequently crashed in the Comoros islands killing all but 52 of the 175 passengers and crew.

MEDITERRANEAN SEA, OFF TURKEY

OCTOBER 12, 1967

When an airliner explodes in the air with the loss of all on board, it can often be difficult to establish the cause of the explosion. This was the case with the British European Airways de Havilland Comet 4B.

British European Airways was one of the first operators of the de Havilland Comet 4B, which it first put into service in May 1952.

In the darkness of early morning on October 12, 1967, one of their Comet fleet took off from London Heathrow airport on a flight to Athens, Greece. Having completed the first leg, the aircraft left Athens for Nicosia on the island of Cyprus, about 559 miles (900km) to the west. The last communication with the aircraft was at 0718 hours, when it was flying on a westbound heading at a height of 29,000 feet (8839m).

At around 0730 hours the Comet was crippled by an explosion. Out of control, the aircraft tumbled 14,000 feet (5,000m) before the fuselage broke into two parts. The wreckage hit the water of the western Mediterranean about 100 miles (150km) east south east of Rhodes. The bodies of 59 of the 66 passengers and crew were recovered, but the depth of water in the region hampered the operation to salvage the wreckage.

At first it was thought the Comet had suffered a structural failure, but when one of the seat cushions was recovered from the water and analysed it was found to contain traces of an unidentified high explosive. Terrorist activity was immediately suspected, particularly in view of the continuing conflict over the sovereignty of Cyprus, in which Britain was taking an active military role.

One theory suggested that a bomb had been placed on board in an attempt to assassinate the leader of the Greek forces in Cyprus, after he had mistakenly been identified as one of the passengers. Another theory was that the bombing was part of an insurance fraud – at least two of the passengers had unusually high cover. But no firm evidence for either theory was ever forthcoming – and the cause of the explosion has never been fully established, nor the killers apprehended.

Below: A BEA de Havilland Comet 4B airliner similar to the one that crashed in the Mediterranean on October 12, 1967 with the loss of all lives.

SIBERIA, RUSSIA
MAY 18, 1973

Above: A Tupolev T-104 jetliner sitting on the tarmac. The hijack of a T-104 in the 1970s was the first occasion that a hijacking resulted in a crash killing all those on board – including the hijacker.

As with so many aspects of life in the former Soviet Union, the details of this disaster are shrouded in secrecy. The incident has the doubtful distinction of being the first occasion that a hijack resulted in a fatal crash. That it took place behind the Iron Curtain illustrates the fact that during the 1970s no country or people were safe from the air pirate.

The Tupolev T-104 was the first jet airliner to emerge from the Soviet Union and was introduced in September 1956. In May 1973 a Tupolev T-104A – one of Aeroflot's veteran fleet of T-104 jetliners – took off on a scheduled flight from Moscow to Chita, about 2920 miles (4700km) to the east. About 1500 miles (2400km) into the flight, the aircraft was at its cruising altitude of approximately 30,000 feet (10,000m) when the hijacker caught the attention of one of the cabin crew and announced that he was carrying an explosive device. He demanded that the jetliner reroute to China. His choice of destination, from one Communist regime to another that was, if anything, even harsher, was curious. If he had landed in China, he would surely have been extradited to Russia.

Neither the hijacker nor his 80 victims reached their planned destinations. The Soviet newspaper *Pravda* reported next day that somewhere east of Lake Baikal the jetliner was fatally crippled when the hijacker decided to detonate the device. From that altitude, the chances of anyone surviving were infinitesimal.

JOHOR BAHARU, MALAYSIA

DECEMBER 4, 1977

The perpetrator of this crime was clearly mentally unbalanced. There can be no other explanation for his actions, which resulted in his death and, more importantly, the death of 100 innocent people. The Boeing 737 that was destroyed in this incident was one of the fleet operated by Malaysian Airlines on internal routes. It took off from Pinang in the north west of Malaysia on a scheduled flight to the capital, Kuala Lumpar, some 190 miles (305km) to the south.

The flight proceeded without incident until the flight crew were making their approach to Kuala Lumpar. At this point a man brandishing a revolver forced his way onto the flight deck and, threatening the pilot, demanded that the aircraft proceed to Johor Baharu, the airport serving Singapore. The crew followed his instructions to the letter. Even so, as the Boeing approached Johor Baharu the hijacker shot and killed both the captain and first officer, the only two people on board capable of flying the aircraft. Pitching out of control into a near vertical dive, the aircraft impacted in a swamp about 30 miles (50km) southwest of Johor Baharu, exploded and broke up. There were no survivors among the 93 passengers and seven crew.

The incident threw a harsh spotlight onto security procedures at Pinang, and led to many questions being asked as to how the hijacker had been able to smuggle a weapon onto the aircraft. It has often been the case that security on internal flights is much laxer than on international routes. On this occasion it proved to be tragically inadequate.

Below: A Boeing 737 belonging to Malaysia-Singapore Airlines – similar to the aircraft that was hijacked and crashed on December 4, 1977.

SEA OF JAPAN, OFF SAKHALIN ISLAND

SEPTEMBER 1, 1983

Below: A Korean Airlines Boeing 747 in flight. It was an airliner similar to this one that was shot down by a Soviet jet fighter on September 1, 1983.

During the Cold War between the US and the USSR there were many incidents involving incursions into enemy airspace that were never reported in the press. Both sides were unwilling to admit that they were conducting highly secret reconnaissance missions by overflying each other's territory. These missions resulted in a number of hostile engagements and established a situation of extreme tension in the air that resulted eventually in the tragedy of Korean Airlines Flight 007.

On September 1, 1983, the cat and mouse game that had been played in the skies for decades resulted in the downing of a commercial airliner and the loss of 269 lives. A Korean Airlines Boeing 747, designated Flight 007, left JFK airport in New York at 0420 hours GMT with 240 passengers and 29 airline staff on board. It was on a scheduled flight to the jetliner's base in Seoul, South Korea.

The aircraft landed to refuel at Anchorage in Alaska and took off again without incident. At this point the flight crew should have entered fresh data into the trio of inertial navigation systems on the flight deck. These work in conjunction with the autopilot to steer the aircraft on the correct course to its destination. However, at 1310 hours and only 10 minutes into the final leg of its journey the 747 began to deviate from its designated course, and onto one that ultimately led it to pass into Soviet airspace.

The Soviet Air Force was placed on full alert, and interceptor aircraft were scrambled into the area the Korean airliner was overflying. This area was the Kamchatka peninsula, one of the most sensitive Soviet

Right: Japanese fishermen attempting to retrieve pieces of the 747's wreckage with fishing nets.

Below: In Seoul, South Korea, bereaved relatives weep as they burn incense before an altar at a memorial service for the 269 people killed when the 747 was shot down.

Pacific Fleet ballistic missile submarine bases. This fact makes the actions of the Soviet defence forces understandable, if not justifiable.

The failure of the Soviet planes to locate the airliner in the darkness did nothing to alleviate the growing tension on the ground. As the Boeing 747 began to approach Sakhalin Island, another highly sensitive Soviet military base in the Sea of Japan, the tension on the ground reached fever pitch.

At 1805 hours GMT, as the dawn rose over the Pacific, the pilot of a Sukhoi Su-15 jet fighter verified on radio that he had made visual contact with the errant jetliner (whose passengers were asleep and totally unaware of the seriousness of their situation). Later examination of voice-data recordings revealed that at no point did the Soviet pilot indicate that the aircraft was in fact a commercial passenger plane.

The Soviet pilot shadowed the airliner for a period of approximately 20 minutes, and attempted to draw the attention of the flight crew with standard IFF (identification friend or foe) code procedures. As a last ditch effort, he fired a burst of cannon fire ahead of the flight deck. After failing to elicit any response he launched two air-to-air missiles, one of which impacted on the airliner's left wing. The crippled aircraft, flying at over 30,000 feet (9000m), experienced a rapid cabin decompression and went into a steep dive. No one stood a chance of surviving the impact, which occurred roughly 52 miles (86km) off Sakhalin Island.

The Soviet authorities did little to aid either the process of recovering the wreckage or that of establishing how such a tragedy could have occurred. Instead they blamed the incident on a combination of US military aggression and Japanese air traffic control incompetence. It was later confirmed that a US Air Force RC-135 reconnaissance aircraft, similar in appearance to the Boeing 747, was operating in the area that night.

Two theories have been put forward as to why the aircraft deviated from its designated route. The first was that the crew failed to set the autopilot correctly on leaving Anchorage. The second was that the flight crew had inputted data that was incorrect by 10° into the inertial navigation system. This last theory would accord with the heading that the aircraft was on when it was shot down.

There is no doubt, however, that procedures and regulations in all quarters were given less than the required attention. And the fact that the Soviet pilot and defence forces failed to make sufficient information available in the aftermath of the tragedy led to widespread condemnation.

Below: The Korean Airlines Boeing 747 was shot down by a Soviet Sukhoi Su-15 jet fighter similar to the one shown here.

ATLANTIC OCEAN, OFF IRELAND

JUNE 23, 1985

When an Air-India Boeing 747 blew up in the air off the coast of Ireland in 1985, all 329 people aboard were killed. This major air disaster was the result of a series of mistakes and security lapses that had made sabotage possible.

The bomb that killed 329 people was almost certainly planted by a Sikh extremist in retaliation for the massacre by the Indian Army of Sikh worshippers at the Golden Temple, Amritsar, in the Punjab region of northern India.

The device was hidden in a suitcase and was probably placed on a Canadian Pacific aircraft designated as Flight CP60 at Vancouver. The man who made the reservation and checked in the suitcase requested that his luggage be transferred to Flight 182, the doomed Air India 747, at Toronto – the destination of Flight CP60. A passenger with his surname also checked in at the same desk that day, with a single item of luggage, which was placed on Flight CP003 to Tokyo, Japan.

At Toronto, all the luggage being transferred from the Canadian Pacific aircraft to the Air-India Boeing should have been scrutinized with X-ray equipment and by random searches. Instead, due to the X-ray equipment being out of order, the luggage was screened by a hand-held electronic device that can, in theory, detect the presence of explosives. However, in this case it obviously failed to do so. Another lapse in security, and one that contravened airline policy, was

Below: An Air-India Boeing 747 flying over mountainous terrain.

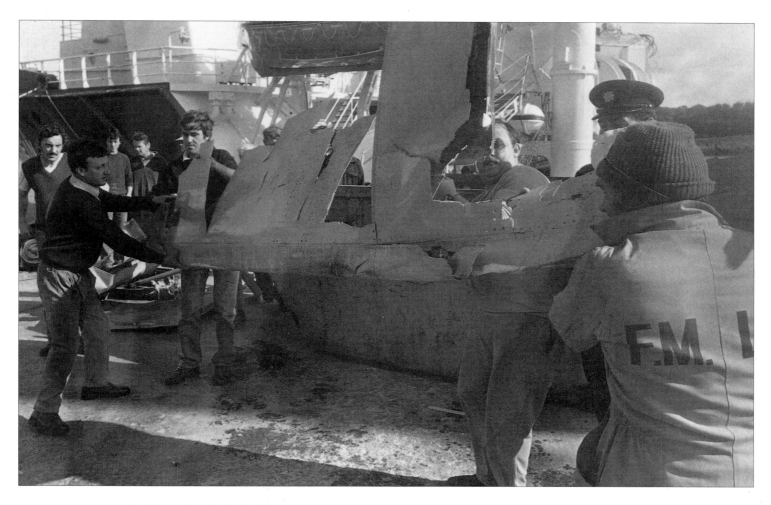

Above: Part of the wreckage from the crashed Air-India Boeing 747 being brought ashore at Foynes, Ireland, from a Norwegian freighter. All wreckage from the aircraft was taken to Cork for investigation.

Right: Officials from Air-India examining some of the wreckage on board the Irish naval vessel Aisling moored at Cork, Ireland.

the failure of airline staff to match passengers to their luggage. An unaccompanied piece of luggage was allowed on the plane.

The saboteur never boarded the aircraft. At 0715 hours in the morning of June 23, in clear skies above the North Atlantic, his murderous device exploded in the forward cargo hold of the Air-India 747. The rapid decompression that follows when the pressurized fuselage of an aircraft flying at height is holed killed many passengers, and probably also caused the flight crew to collapse unconscious at the controls as they battled to save the stricken jumbo. Wreckage was strewn over a large area, and 95 percent of it sank without a trace into the Atlantic. Only 132 bodies were retrieved from the sea – there were no survivors.

Approximately an hour before the Air-India Boeing exploded, a second device contained in the luggage the man had placed on Flight CP003 exploded prematurely while being transferred to Air-India Flight 301 at Narita airport in Tokyo. Two people were killed. But for an incorrectly set timer in this second device, the death toll would almost certainly have been much higher.

After seven years of extensive investigation the police arrested a 30-year-old man they believed to be responsible for the bombings.

PERSIAN GULF

There are always risks attached to operating commercial transport aircraft in airspace adjacent to a war zone. In a war zone military personnel are operating in a heightened state of tension, and are forced to make split-second decisions that can – and do – lead to mistakes. The fate of Iran Air's Flight 655 demonstrates how a case of mistaken identity can end in tragedy.

The Persian Gulf during 1988 was an extremely hostile environment. The Iran-Iraq War had been raging since 1979, and had become a war of attrition. During the mid-1980s both sides had taken to attacking commercial shipping sailing in the Gulf, with the intention of denying vital oil supplies to the enemy.

To protect the oil it buys from Kuwait, the US committed part of the Fifth Fleet to the troubled region in May 1987 to escort vulnerable Kuwaiti tankers, which were forced to sail almost the entire length of the Gulf and through the narrow jaws of the Strait of Hormuz. A matter of days after the fleet was on station, the lives of 37 US sailors were lost when an Iraqi Air Force Mirage attacked the USS *Stark*, supposedly by accident. As a result of this tragedy US commanders were effectively given revised rules of engagement to enable them to defend US military personnel and equipment against acts of aggression.

A year on from the deployment, on Sunday July 3, 1988, the US frigate *Vincennes* became engaged in a surface battle with Iranian gunboats in the Strait of Hormuz. Fully alerted to the possibility of an air strike, and with the *Stark* incident fresh in their minds, the crew of the *Vincennes* positively identified a radar echo emanating from the coastal area of Iran as an F-14 Tomcat, an aircraft which, ironically enough, the Americans had sold to Iran in the early 1980s. The aircraft was given a series of warnings on both the international air defence and military air distress radio frequencies – standard procedure in such situations.

Captain Rogers of the *Vincennes* was faced with a stark choice. His vessel was maneuvering violently while engaging with the Iranian ships. At the same time an aircraft confirmed as a military type by his air defence officer was apparently closing on his position. His decision to launch two surface-to-air missiles to counter the threat was perhaps a result of the pressures he was facing, and one that many people in his position would have made.

The passengers and crew of Flight 655 probably never knew what hit them. The aircraft wrongly identified as a fighter aircraft was in fact an Iranian jetliner – an Airbus A300. It had taken off from Bander Abbas, a city on the southwestern coast of Iran, at approximately 1015 hours with 278 passengers and 12 crew bound for Dubai, UAE, about 155 miles (250km) to the southwest. Only 20 minutes after take-off everyone on board was dead.

At a speed approaching 1900mph (3000km/h), the effect of a standard surface-to-air missile impacting on a wide bodied jet would have been catastrophic. About 70 percent of the bodies and a large quantity of wreck-

Above: An Iran Air Airbus A300 similar to the one shot down in the Persian Gulf by the US frigate Vincennes.

Above: The radar screens on board the Vincennes. *Information from these screens indicated to the captain that the Iran Air Airbus was a hostile aircraft.*

age were recovered from the waters of the Gulf. The large area over which the remains were spread suggests that the aircraft broke up in mid-air.

Inquiries were launched immediately by the US Navy, the Iranian government, and the independent International Civil Aviation Organization. The most crucial evidence came from tape recordings of the air defence radar on the *Vincennes*, which clearly showed that the Iranian Airbus had registered a transponder code identifying it as a civilian aircraft. A transponder emits a coded electronic signal that shows up on a radar screen as a series of numbers. A Mode II signal is used by military aircraft, Mode III by civil aircraft. Another anomaly was revealed by the data transcript, which showed that the airliner was climbing at the time of the impact, while the information given to the captain approximately 90 seconds before his fatal decision was that the aircraft was rapidly descending.

Further investigations revealed that as both civilian and military air fleets were operating out of Bander Abbas at the time, the Airbus had been confused with the transponder emission from an F-14 as it took off. Although the US Navy gave its full backing to Captain Rogers and his crew, the captain of a US naval vessel also involved in the surface battle on the day of the tragedy criticized Rogers and his officers for their openly aggressive actions.

Above: The USS Vincennes, *which was engaged in a surface battle with Iranian gunboats at the time of the incident.*

21

LOCKERBIE, SCOTLAND

DECEMBER 21, 1988

At 2000 hours on December 21, 1988, members of the British Air Accidents Investigations Branch (AAIB) were racing to the small town of Lockerbie in Dumfrieshire, Scotland, to begin the harrowing task of piecing together the last moments of Pan American Flight 103 bound from London to New York.

The scene that greeted them in the sleepy town was one of widespread devastation. Wreckage from the Boeing 747-121 had plummeted into the southern edge of the town, gouging a huge crater more than 155 feet (47m) long in the residential area of Sherwood Crescent. A 60-feet (18-m) section of the rear fuselage had also crashed into a residential block about 2000 feet (600m) away. Debris and wreckage were scattered along two mains paths, and were recovered from 80 miles (130km) away down the east coast of England. There were no survivors among the 259 people on board the aircraft. The fact that there were only 11 fatalities among the residents of Lockerbie is nothing short of miraculous.

From the manner of the violent destruction of the aircraft it soon became clear to the investigative teams that the jumbo had been ripped apart by some sort of explosion while at altitude. Within a few days items of wreckage were recovered from which forensic scientists found clear evidence of the use of a sinister high

Below: The devastation in the small Scottish town of Lockerbie, caused by wreckage from the Pan Am Boeing 747 crashing into a residential block.

Right: *Part of the wrecked cockpit of the crashed Boeing 747 being examined by investigators.*

Below: *The forward section of the fuselage of the crashed plane was found in a field about 2.5 miles (4km) east of Lockerbie.*

explosive – Semtex – which is a favoured tool of the terrorist. The investigation then developed into a murder hunt.

The Pan American Boeing had arrived at London Heathrow Airport from San Francisco in the late morning of December 21. The aircraft was routinely cleaned and resupplied in preparation for its return flight across the Atlantic to New York's JFK airport. It was scheduled to depart at 1800 hours that evening.

Boarding the plane for the transAtlantic flight were 49 passengers, together with their baggage, who had transferred from a flight that originated in Frankfurt, West Germany. In addition to these 49, another 194 passengers boarded, together with 16 members of the flight and cabin crew. At 1825 hours the Boeing took off and adopted a northwesterly course, heading through the center of Britain, and climbing to an altitude of 31,000 feet (9449m). At 1858 hours an air traffic controller at Shanwick (now Prestwick) Oceanic Area Control (the coordinating traffic control for transatlantic flights) transmitted a message to the Pan Am flight crew, confirming their clearance for the flight over the North Atlantic. When the message was not acknowledged, and the radar echo from Flight 103 broke up on their screens, officers at air traffic control began to fear the worst.

Residents in Lockerbie reported hearing a rumbling noise like thunder, which steadily grew louder like the

Above: A fireman searching the debris in the town caused by the impact of the disintegrating Boeing 747. Houses and cars were destroyed, but only 11 residents of Lockerbie were killed.

roar of a jet engine. Rushing to their windows, many of them saw the flaming hulk of the plane's fuselage, and the wing, crashing to the ground.

Approximately 90 percent of the wreckage was recovered – scattered over a wide area – during the course of the next 14 days. It was taken to a British Army base near Lockerbie. The forward section of the fuselage, which was recovered largely intact from a field about 2.5 miles (4km) east of the town, was reconstructed at the accident facility of the Royal Aircraft Establishment at Farnborough in England.

After many months of painstaking investigation, involving explosives experts, terrorist counter-intelligence experts, and members of the AAIB and the US National Transportation Safety Board, a preliminary report was published.

The detonation of an explosive device concealed in a Toshiba radio cassette recorder in the cargo hold had ruptured the pressurized hull of the aircraft, causing an explosive decompression, loss of control, and disintegration of the jetliner.

Embedded in a piece of luggage the investigators had found a tiny fragment of a Swiss timing device. The accusing eyes of the world turned on Libya when it was revealed that this same device had been sold to that country in 1985. The criminal investigation revealed that the device, contained in the baggage of a 50-year-old Libyan man, had been transferred from Air Malta Flight 180 at Frankfurt onto a Boeing 727, and then onto the Pan American flight.

The two Libyan terrorists accused of the murder of the Lockerbie victims remain at the center of a legal and political wrangle as to where they should stand trial. In the immediate aftermath of the bombing it was speculated that the crime was carried out in retaliation for the downing of the Iran Air Airbus in the Persian Gulf six months previously. The focus of attention was on the Libyan government, who were believed to have provided financial and logistical support for the operation to avenge the US air strikes against Tripoli in 1986. Whatever the reasons, 10 years after the disaster, no one had been brought to justice.

BOGOTA, COLOMBIA

NOVEMBER 27, 1989

Colombia is riddled with illegal drug cartels that are an agonizing thorn in the country's side. The leaders of these rackets and the killers that they employ have inflicted acts of terror on Colombian society for years. The Colombian judiciary and police agencies are the prime target, but many other innocent people have been caught in the crossfire. In 1989 a brutal act of terror was committed in the air that left the country reeling in shock, and which highlighted the need for diligent security at both national and international airports throughout the world.

On November 27, 1989, a Boeing 727-21 of Aerovias Nacionales de Colombia (AVIANCA) took off from Bogota's El Dorado airport on a scheduled flight to Cali, about 193 miles (310km) to the south west. Among the passengers were five police informers, who between them had information that could have led to the conviction of some of Colombia's most infamous cocaine barons. They were closely guarded, and known to be under a death sentence from the cartels.

Five minutes after leaving the ground the Boeing was ripped apart by an explosion. The burning aircraft plunged to the earth and impacted on a hillside, instan-

Below: Rescue workers recovering the body of the pilot of the Avianca aircraft. The Boeing 727 crashed into a hillside shortly after take-off killing all on board.

Right: The remains of the Avianca Boeing after it exploded and crashed on November 27, 1989.

Below: Rescue workers removing the body of one of the victims from the scene of the crash.

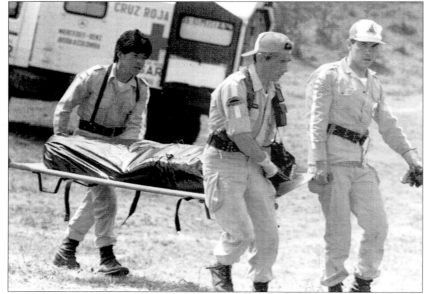

Far right: A Colombian air force specialist searches for evidence in the debris as to what may have caused the crash.

mid-point of the passenger cabin. This had ruptured the main fuel tank under the cabin floor causing the highly inflammable aviation fuel to engulf the rear fuselage. The explosion probably also severed crucial control wires.

Police investigations have never succeeded in identifying the individual who planted the device on the aircraft. However, the senior cartel member who was widely believed to have been responsible for this act of sabotage was shot and killed by police during a raid in 1992.

taneously killing anyone who might have survived the explosion and resulting decompression. Rescue workers succeeded in recovering 110 bodies, including those of three unidentified people. These were not on the passenger list, which is supposed to provide an accurate record of all those on board. It is possible that these were the bodies of people on the ground who were killed by the aircraft.

Subsequent investigations into the crash revealed that an explosive device had detonated in a position on the right-hand side of the aircraft, somewhere near the

COMOROS ISLAND, MADAGASCAR

NOVEMBER 23, 1996

Above: The remains of the Ethiopian Boeing 767 resting on a reef off the island of Comoros in the Indian Ocean. Rescuers found 55 survivors, including two of the terrorists, who were arrested.

The pilot of an Ethiopian Boeing 767, Captain Levl Abate, was honored by the Guild of Airline Pilots in October, 1997, for the considerable bravery and skill that he showed when his aircraft was hijacked by three terrorists.

Ethiopian Airlines Flight 961 was on a scheduled service from Ethiopia to Kenya when the hijackers burst onto the flight deck. Their demands were unclear, and the aircraft circled helplessly for a considerable length of time while the pilot tried unsuccessfully to reason with them.

The aircraft was flying in a southeasterly direction, but was soon in danger of running out of fuel. The pilot was forced to attempt a landing near Moroni, but as he approached a struggle developed on the flight deck. During the ensuing fight, both engines failed due to lack of fuel, and there was a total loss of the hydraulic power necessary to control the aircraft. At a point only some 900 feet (275m) off Le Galawa beach, and in full view of tourists (one of whom recorded the event on a cam-corder), the aircraft skimmed over a calm sea and then banked to the left, causing the port wing to touch in the wave tops. Moments later, the port engine also dragged in the water, spinning the aircraft around, and causing it to break behind the wing. Some of the passengers were thrown out by the momentum.

Onlookers and local fishermen helped shocked and dazed survivors to the shore, but 120 of the 175 people on board were killed.

HUMAN ERROR

A heavy burden of responsibility lies with those who fly and maintain aircraft. Whether the aircraft is a microlight, a jet fighter, or a jumbo jet, everyone concerned with flying or maintaining it needs to act with professionalism and to pay constant attention to detail if the skies are to remain safe.

Every human being is susceptible to lapses of concentration at some time and is liable to make mistakes. Pilots, technicians, and air traffic control staff are no different from other people, and no amount of professional training and experience can ever totally remove human failing. Although the application of technology has eased many of the pilot's tasks, flying the vastly complex aircraft of today will always be a demanding job. The simple truth is that a large number of aircraft accidents are directly attributable to mistakes made by the flight crew during the two most crucial stages of any flight – take-off and landing. Fortunately, the rigorous selection and training that professional pilots undergo make such accidents a rare occurrence. But overfamiliarity with procedures and techniques, pressures of maintaining a schedule, or fatigue do sometimes lead flight crews to overlook basic safety procedures, or simply to flip the wrong switch.

Right: The wreckage of the BEA Trident that crashed in 1972 in a field near Staines, England, almost immediately after taking off from Heathrow airport. There were no survivors.

SIGGINSTON, WALES

MARCH 12, 1950

Avro's Tudor aircraft was one of the earliest airliners. It was developed and first put into service in the mid 1940s. Its history was marred by several crashes, one of which killed its designer, Roy Chadwick. On March 12, 1950, another Tudor V aircraft crashed with a party of Welsh rugby football supporters on board.

The crash of the Tudor V was due to errors both by the ground crew, and by the pilot failing to make adequate preflight checks regarding the correct distribution of weight in the aircraft.

The aircraft was chartered by a group of Welsh rugby fans to ferry them to Dublin in Ireland, where they watched Wales beat Ireland in the international match at Belfast. On the day following the Welsh victory, the jubilant fans boarded the aircraft at Dublin for the homeward flight back to Llandow airport, serving Cardiff.

For the return flight, six more passengers had been added to the manifest. Crucially, although the seating arrangements had been altered – thus affecting the balance of the aircraft – the luggage in the hold was neither sufficiently heavy, nor properly distributed, to correct the centre of gravity.

At about 1445 hours, as the aircraft was making its final approach to Llandow, observers on the ground realized that it was in trouble. When the Tudor was over the runway centre line at a height of about 120 feet (37m) the pilot tried to correct his angle of descent (which investigators adjudged to have been too steep) by applying full power. However, because the poor distribution of weight had resulted in a rearward shift of the centre of gravity, this action made the aircraft difficult to control.

The Tudor climbed rapidly to a height of about 300 feet (100m), stalled, and crashed into a field, coming to rest only 20 yards (18m) from a farmhouse in the little village of Sigginston. Although there was no explosion, the impact killed all 83 of those on board.

Left: The scene just outside the village of Sigginston, South Wales, the day after the Avro Tudor V crashed while making its final approach for landing at Llandow airport.

EAST RIVER, NEW YORK, USA

FEBRUARY 3, 1959

Right: A rescue boat searching for victims of the Lockheed Electra crash. Of the 73 people on board 65 died when the aircraft failed to make an instrument landing at La Guardia airport at night and crashed into the East River.

Below: A giant derrick on a salvage boat lifts the tail section of the wrecked plane out of the river.

Among the eight survivors of this accident was an eight-year-old boy returning from Chicago with his mother, father, and two sisters. He was the only one of them to be rescued alive. Many of the victims survived the impact into the chilly waters of the East River, only to drown as they struggled to escape the rapidly sinking wreckage. Accident investigators were able to piece together an intricate picture of the errors leading to the crash from the accounts of the first and second officers, both of whom survived.

The Lockheed Electra airliner, belonging to American Airlines, was coming to the end of an internal flight from Chicago, Illinois, 730 miles (1174km) to the west. Although the flight crew had many years of air experience between them on a number of different aircraft types, they had only limited hours on the Electra, which had entered service with the airline less than two weeks earlier.

The weather conditions at La Guardia airport – the destination of the turboprop airliner – were poor, with visibility down to two miles (3km), low cloud base at only 350 feet (110m) and light rain and fog.

The conditions gave the flight crew little option but to make an approach based on instrument readings and the instrument landing system (ILS). This allows the aircraft to be guided to the ground by following a lateral heading beam and another angled vertical beam – both beams transmitted by ground-based navigational aids. The crew of the Electra were not familiar with an ILS landing at La Guardia, and as they approached the airport, they were under considerable pressure both to carry out the routine tasks of lowering the undercarriage and extending the flaps, and also to cope with the unfamiliar landing system.

There was little the flight crew could do to prevent the crash, which happened only seconds after the aircraft broke out of the dense overcast. The aircraft plowed into the icy East River, 5000 feet (1520m) away from Runway 22, where it should have landed. But for the presence of the tugboat *Dorothy McAllister* close by, it is doubtful whether anyone at all on the aircraft would have survived.

The US Civil Aeronautics Board, who investigated the crash, made serious criticisms of the captain and his two officers, and also airline operating practices. Instruments salvaged from the wreckage – much of which was recovered from the depths of the East River – showed potentially fatal anomalies. The altimeter had been inaccurately set at Chicago, and was reading nearly 120 feet (36m) too high. Added to this, the first officer, whose responsibilities included making regular reports to the captain on the aircraft's speed and altitude, was distracted by the complications and unfamiliar procedures of the instrument landing system at La Guardia.

These two errors on the part of the flight crew, combined with their unfamiliarity with the aircraft, were deemed to have caused the crash. Evidence given to the Civil Aeronautics Board by the two junior flight officers indicated that the design of the instruments confused them; this may have led to mistaken instrument readings. In addition, there was inadequate approach lighting to Runway 22, and the rain and poor visibility may have combined to give the pilot the impression that he was higher than he really was.

Left: *A marine crane lifts wreckage from the Electra onto a barge. Many of the bodies of the victims of the disaster were never recovered from the river.*

STAINES, ENGLAND

JUNE 18, 1972

The major reason for the crash of BEA Hawker Siddeley Trident on June 18, 1972, was the failure of the flight crew to make rational and effective decisions when a serious problem occurred during one of the most critical stages of any flight – take-off.

Below: Police and firemen survey the smoldering wreckage of the BEA Trident that crashed into a field in Staines shortly after take-off from Heathrow airport.

Although at 51 he was by no means an old man, the BEA pilot Stanley Key was by all indications not in prime physical condition. Six months prior to the crash he had undergone electrocardiogram screening and been passed fit to fly by medical examiners of the British Civilian Air Authority, yet the autopsy carried out on his body after the disaster showed that the arteries around his heart were severely restricted.

The Trident was due to make a scheduled flight from London's Heathrow airport to Brussels, Belgium. One element in the sequence of events that led to the tragedy can be traced back to the flight crew restroom at Heathrow, where Key became involved in a heated argument with a fellow pilot. The coroner concluded that the rise in blood pressure that this would have caused damaged one of the arteries of his heart.

By the time he boarded the aircraft he was probably in great pain. Both his first and second officers were in their early twenties, with far less experience than their captain, and were undoubtedly reluctant to question his command. Once the 112 passengers (almost the maximum capacity of the Trident) were seated and briefed, the flight crew proceeded as normal with their

Left: The fuselage of the crashed plane reassembled at the Royal Aircraft Establishment, Farnborough, where it was taken for investigation.

preflight preparations. The aircraft, given the call sign "Papa India", was cleared for take-off, and at approximately 1709 hours lifted off from Runway 28R at Heathrow.

Laboratory research has shown that all pilots experience a rise in heart rate at this point in a flight – this would have put further stress on Key's heart, probably causing him extreme discomfort, and this provides part of the explanation for the tragedy.

Only 75 seconds into the flight, one of the flight crew (most probably the captain), retracted the lift-assisting devices positioned on the leading edge of the wing. The Trident was, however, only traveling at 70 percent of the prescribed speed necessary for this action. The crew then reduced thrust, and retracted the lift-enhancing flaps on the trailing edge of the wing. With the Trident's insufficient airspeed the combination of these actions caused the aircraft to become dangerously unstable, but not critically so.

Although the aircraft was approaching a stall, the "stick-shaker" would have provided the crew with sufficient warning to lower the nose and redeploy the droops.

The Trident was one of the first aircraft to be fitted with the stick-shaker, which, as its name suggests, is a device that shakes the control column if the aircraft is approaching a stall. Later analysis showed that after it activated a second time, the device on Key's flight deck was manually overridden. Many Trident crews had expressed their dissatisfaction with the system, reporting that it was prone to engage unecessarily. Someone on the flight deck of "Papa India" must have assumed incorrectly that the device was malfunctioning and switched it off.

Less than two minutes into the flight, the Trident entered an unrecoverable stall at a height of about 1970 feet (600m). It impacted at a relatively shallow angle in a field 3 miles (5km) southwest of the runway threshold, having narrowly missed a major trunk road packed with homebound commuters. There was no explosion, and the automatic extinguishing system rapidly doused a fire that erupted. Tragically, there were no survivors among the 118 bodies pulled from the wreckage.

Unfortunately, there was no cockpit flight recorder installed on the Trident, which despite the crash remained largely intact. This added to the difficult task the air accident investigators faced when trying to explain the deaths of the 118 people on board.

Since that time, it has become almost routine for a cockpit flight recorder to be installed on the flight deck of a commercial airliner and the absence of it would now be considered negligence on the part of the airline. This is one more indication of how air safety improves after a disaster.

TENERIFE, CANARY ISLANDS, SPAIN

DECEMBER 3, 1972

Below: The island of Tenerife, which is a popular destination for Europeans on vacation. It was a charter flight full of German tourists that crashed fatally on take-off from the island's airport.

There was a huge increase in the volume of air traffic operating in and out of Tenerife during the early 1970s, due to the growing popularity of the island as a destination for Europeans on vacation, particularly from West Germany and the UK. During the winter months, when this accident occurred, the mild weather attracts countless numbers of sun seekers, and the volume of traffic remains correspondingly high.

The Spantax aircraft – a Coronado – was on a charter service scheduled to take off from Los Rodeos airport in the early dawn (an inconvenience that will be familiar to anyone who has ever taken a charter flight) bound for Munich in West Germany. Low overcast was covering the island, but weather conditions were not deemed serious enough to warrant suspending normal operations. In the previous six years Spantax had suffered two fatal accidents in the Canaries with the loss of 33 lives. In this tragedy more than 150 were to perish.

The Coronado took off at 0645 hours, climbed to a height of only 300 feet (100m), and then plunged to the ground. The fuselage came to rest in an inverted position. All 148 passengers, most of them German tourists, were killed together with the flight and cabin crew of seven Spaniards.

It was later concluded by the investigating Spanish authority that the pilot had lost control of the aircraft at about the point when the nosewheel left the ground. It proved difficult to pinpoint the exact reason why he experienced this loss of control, a problem that occurs in a considerable number of aircraft accidents that are attributed to human errors.

The most likely conclusion is that the pilot became disorientated in conditions of almost zero visibility. With the benefit of hindsight, his decision to take off when he was fully aware of the poor weather conditions might be thought questionable. That said, airline pilots are often under quite considerable pressures to maintain their schedules. All the time that commercial aircraft are sitting on the ground they are losing money for their operators, and this is clearly undesirable in a fiercely competitive business. These commercial pressures inevitably filter down to the captain, who is caught in the conflict between the profitability of his airline and the safety of his aircraft, passengers, and crew.

Above: The remains of the victims of the Coronado crash are loaded on to stretchers by Red Cross workers.

Right: The wreckage of the chartered Coronado airliner that crashed just after its dawn take-off, killing all on board.

ROSS ISLAND, ANTARCTICA

NOVEMBER 28, 1979

The report of the commission set up to investigate this tragedy, which was to date New Zealand's worst ever air disaster, made scathing attacks on both the carrier and the flight crew. Both parties certainly made disastrous errors of judgment that turned what had been planned as a pleasant sight-seeing trip over the stunning landscape of the Ross Ice Shelf in Antarctica into a catastrophe.

Flying in the Antarctic requires constant vigilance, highly developed skill, and precise judgment, both to predict and safely assess the often hostile weather conditions, and also to navigate successfully without the benefit of obvious ground reference points. Another complication is that magnetic compasses are rendered useless in Antarctica because of the existence of powerful magnetic fields around the South Pole.

Left: Antarctica may be stunningly beautful when seen from the safety of the air, but in reality it is a desolate, inhospitable wasteland of ice and frozen seas. It was in a landscape like this that the McDonnell Douglas DC-10 crashed in November 1979.

The flight officers of the Air New Zealand McDonnell Douglas DC-10 were given a briefing prior to the flight, which was later judged to have been insufficiently detailed. Only one of the five officers had made such a flight before. During preflight preparations at Auckland, one of the crew inputted a detailed flight plan into the inertial navigation system on the DC-10. This plots a flight profile and is used to calculate the position of the aircraft and where possible cross-references with land-based navigation aids.

Investigations later revealed that this data was wrong. It was based on incorrect information that Air New Zealand aircraft had been using for at least 14 months. However, as all previous sight-seeing trips had been made in conditions of far greater visibility than on the day of the fatal crash, the flight crews would not have been forced to rely heavily on their instruments, as was the situation on this day.

As he approached Ross Island, which lies at the edge of the Antarctic ice cap, south-west of New Zealand's South Island, the pilot decided to descend below the base of the low, dense overcast, to facilitate better viewing for the passengers.

This was a reckless violation of the guidelines, which strictly forbade flying below 6000 feet (1800m) until the mountain range that was now lying directly in the path of the airliner had been passed.

The error in the inertial navigation system data also meant that the aircraft was some 30 miles (50km) off course and on a track headed toward the towering peak of Mount Erebus.

Flying in thick cloud the flight crew could see nothing of the approaching danger, and decided to descend to 1500 feet (500m). As the aircraft emerged from the dense overcast, visibility was still poor, and the crew saw the wall of rock and ice in front of them too late. The aircraft struck a slope on the western approaches to Mount Erebus at nearly 300 mph (483 km/h) killing all 257 persons on board.

Left: The wreckage of the Air New Zealand McDonnell Douglas DC-10 strewn on the snow-covered slopes of Mount Erebus in Antarctica. No one on board survived.

TENERIFE, CANARY ISLANDS, SPAIN

APRIL 25, 1980

Above: A Dan-Air Boeing 727 similar to the ill-fated aircraft that crashed in Tenerife carrying British tourists to the Canary Islands.

Tragedy struck the holiday island of Tenerife yet again on April 25, 1980, this time claiming the lives of 146 people flying in a Dan-Air Boeing 727. The accident highlighted the necessity for a clear and concise system of communication between aircrew and ground controllers. Both the KLM-PanAm collision in 1975, and the destruction of the Dan-Air Boeing 727 were in part attributable to inadequacies in this communication.

Spanish air traffic control came under intense scrutiny during the late 1970s and early 1980s. Many aviation analysts questioned whether the organization possessed either the professionalism or the equipment to cope with the volume of traffic that was operating out of their national airports.

However, given the particular circumstances and the actions of the Dan-Air crew in the minutes prior to this tragedy, it would be unjust to lay too much blame at the door of Spanish air traffic control operatives.

It seems that in this case, mutual incomprehension and casual oversights by human beings combined to create a human catastrophe.

In the late morning of April 25, 146 people (138 passengers and 8 flight and cabin crew) boarded the Dan-Air charter service from Manchester, England, bound for the beaches of Tenerife. The flight was uneventful up until the point where the aircraft passed into the jurisdiction of approach controllers at Los Rodeos airport in Tenerife. The weather conditions in the locality consisted of broken overcast, with a cloud base down to 3000 feet (1000m).

At this point, inaccurate navigation by the crew had resulted in the aircraft being nearly a mile (1.5km) to the east of its correct flight path. The approach controller, who was operating without the benefit of radar, was unclear as to the position of the aircraft and subsequently cleared the crew to descend to 6000 feet (1828m) and to enter a holding pattern in anticipation of a landing slot. The failure of the crew to report their position accurately after crossing over the VOR navigational aid (a ground-based electronic navigational aid) further aggravated the situation.

Further confusion arose when the controller instructed the crew to turn to the left, which in fact would have taken the aircraft away from Los Rodeos airport. This apparently irrational order disorientated the crew for vital seconds. As a result, the crew failed to enter the race track holding pattern over Los Rodeos, and continued flying towards the mountainous area to the southwest of the airport.

The aircraft was flying in cloud at a height of 5500 feet (1660m), when the ground proximity warning system sounded, and almost immediately deactivated as the 727 flew over a valley. The pilot, clearly confused about the location of the high ground, made a rapid evasive movement to the right at this time, but nearly 30 seconds later the ground proximity warning system sounded again. This time there was no opportunity for evasive action. The aircraft slammed into a mountainside and disintegrated, instantly killing all those on board.

Below: Rescue workers search for debris from the Boeing 727 that crashed in the woods south of Los Rodeos airport, Tenerife, killing all 146 passengers and crew.

RIYADH, SAUDI ARABIA

FEBRUARY 19, 1980

Above: The Saudi Arabian airliner in which 301 people burned to death was a Lockheed Tristar like this one.

When the fire alarms indicating smoke in the aft cargo compartment sounded on February 19, 1980, on the flight deck of a Saudi Lockheed Tristar bound for Jiddah in Saudi Arabia, it quickly became obvious that the flight crew had little idea what to do.

The Tristar was only minutes into the second leg of a service from Karachi, Pakistan. The crew, none of whom had much experience on this type of aircraft, delayed four long minutes before confirming the alert, and then – almost unbelievably – had to search for the manual showing the correct procedure in such an incident. Clearly failing to treat the fire with adequate seriousness at this stage, the flight engineer repeatedly suggested that there was "no problem."

In the passenger compartment, the 287 passengers and 10 cabin staff were somewhat more concerned. As smoke seeped into the cabin, the cabin crew struggled to maintain calm. The captain turned back to Riyadh to land. After landing, the captain should have applied full reverse thrust and utilized every means possible to bring the aircraft rapidly to a halt, to allow a fast evacuation of the plane. Instead, he chose to taxi ponderously off the runway, trapping the passengers in the fume-filled aircraft for another 180 seconds. He then continued to run the engines for over three minutes, preventing rescue crews from taking action, and the cabin crew from initiating the evacuation.

As fire swept through the landed Tristar rescuers could only watch helplessly. It was clear that the rescue crews lacked adequate training, equipment, and leadership to deal with such an event. Nearly 30 minutes after the aircraft had returned to Riyadh, they were finally able to cut their way into the wreckage. All 301 people on board were dead, among them 15 babies. In the history of air disasters, it was a costly and needless waste of life almost without equal.

DETROIT, MICHIGAN, USA

AUGUST 16, 1987

The sole survivor of the Northwest Airlines Flight 255 of August 16, 1987, was a four-year-old girl. Tragically, she lost her other three immediate relatives in the accident, which robbed another 153 of their lives.

The US National Transportation Safety Board, which investigates all air accidents in the country, highlighted as the cause of the crash the lack of communication between the captain and his co-pilot while they were conducting take-off procedures at Wayne County Airport at Detroit.

Specifically, the first officer failed to extend the flaps while the aircraft was taxiing just before it was cleared to take-off. The captain also showed a dereliction of duty by failing to complete preflight and take-off checks according to airline procedure.

Without either extended flaps or slats (retractable lifting surfaces on the leading edge of the wing) the McDonnell Douglas DC-9 Super 82 – and indeed any modern commercial transport aircraft – has a greatly reduced climbing capability.

After a ground run of about 6800 feet (2073m) the Northwest Airlines DC-9 lifted off the runway. If the aircraft had been properly configured, it would have been climbing through 600 feet (182m) when it was 4500 feet (1350m) further on its course. In fact, due to the fatal oversight of the flight crew, the aircraft had struggled to an altitude of barely 41 feet (12m). Only 14 seconds into the flight to Phoenix, Arizona, the port (left) wing clipped a string of lamp-posts and a building, and the aircraft plummeted onto a road about half a mile from the end of the runway.

The two occupants of the car that the aircraft also hit were killed instantaneously. As for the occupants of the aircraft, when the emergency teams arrived at the scene of devastation they were amazed to find that one person had survived the crash – a four-year-old girl.

Below: The scene on the highway where the Northwest Airlines DC-9 crashed soon after take-off.

OFF PUERTO PLATA, DOMINICAN REPUBLIC

FEBRUARY 6, 1996

Right: US Coast Guards load debris and wreckage from the crashed Boeing 757 onto the cutter *Knight Island.*

Most of the 176 passengers of Flight 301 were Germans returning from a winter vacation in the Caribbean island of Puerto Plata. The Birgenair Boeing 757 had been chartered by the Dominican airline Alas Nacionales for the flight to Germany via Gander in Canada. The captain began his take-off run at about 2341 hours.

The aircraft accelerated rapidly to 92mph (148km/h) at which point the captain discovered that his ASI (airspeed indicator) was malfunctioning. The co-pilot's indicator seemed to work fine. The aircraft took-off at approximately 2342 hours and began climbing to cruising altitude. As the aircraft was passing through 4700 feet (1433m) the captain's ASI was indicating 403mph (648km/h) – far in excess of the correct climb-out speed. This resulted in an autopilot/autothrottle reaction to increase the nose -up attitude and a power reduction in order to lower the airspeed.

However, the actual speed was only 253mph (408km/h). As the flight management system automatically reduced speed the crew received warnings from the audible warning system (an electronic voice which informs flight crew of potential hazards). Both pilots appear to have become confused when the co-pilot stated that although his ASI read 230mph (370km/h) they were getting an excessive speed warning. This was rapidly followed by a "stickshaker" warning, leading both pilots to believe that both airspeed indicators were unreliable.

Finally realizing that they were losing speed and altitude the pilots disconnected the autopilot (which had reduced the speed close to the stall speed) and applied full thrust. At 17 seconds past 2347 hours an aural ground proximity warning sounded. Eight seconds later the aircraft struck the ocean, about five miles off the coast. All those on board were killed.

In the subsequent investigation it was suggested that poor ground maintenance might have resulted in the malfunctioning of the airspeed indicator. But the crew's failure to react to the stickshaker warning of imminent stall, and their failure to execute the procedures for recovery from the onset of loss of control, were predominantly to blame for the disaster.

COLLISION

Collision in the air is a constant danger. Although air traffic is rigorously controlled and flight paths are strictly laid down by aviation authorities, the possibility of aircaft colliding can never be wholly eradicated. As the volume of traffic flying above our heads to an ever diverse range of destinations increases, so too the danger of collision in the air increases.

One of the first and most catastrophic incidents recorded took place over the Grand Canyon in the USA in the 1950s. This crash highlighted the inedequacies at that time of the system of air traffic control, which had not kept pace with the huge increase in air traffic. The horrific KLM-PanAm collision on the runway at Tenerife some 21 years later demonstrated the need for flight crews to exercise constant vigilance, even on the ground. This incident, the worst in the history of commercial aviation, was the catastrophe that everybody had been dreading since the introduction of widebodied airliners capable of carrying in excess of 500 passengers.

These tragedies remind us that collision is an ever-present danger. Countless incidents are recorded each year involving near-misses between aircraft, and many more probably go unreported.

Right: The aftermath of a collision between a Saudi Arabian jumbo jet and a Kazakhstan airliner near Delhi, India, on November 12, 1996. Both aircraft disintegrated in mid air, scattering wreckage over a wide area.

EMPIRE STATE BUILDING, NEW YORK, USA

JULY 28, 1945

I n July 1945 with the war in Europe over, and the war in the east nearing its end, hundreds of aircraft began to arrive back in the United States from bases abroad. **The United States produced no less than 11,000 B-25 medium bombers during World War II; when the war was over many of these ended their days as research platforms.**

At 0855 hours on the morning of Saturday, July 28, Lt. Col. William Smith, an experienced flier with many hours under his belt, and a highly decorated combat veteran of World War II, took off from Bedford Field aerodrome, north of Boston. At 27 years old, he was one of the youngest lieutenant colonels in the US Air Force, and had a reputation as something of a

Left: *The Empire State Building, New York. The B-25 bomber plane piloted by Lt. Col. William Smith smashed into the 79th floor of the building, causing destruction and havoc to the city's landmark skyscraper.*

Above: One of the 11,000 B-25 medium bombers produced for the United States forces during World War II. It was a B-25 that smashed into the Empire State Building on July 28, 1945.

Right: A US sailor holds up one of the bomber's propellers found in the wreckage.

and this was causing a backlog in incoming traffic. In spite of this Smith decided to proceed and reached New York in about 50 minutes. He was initially refused landing permission because of the volume of traffic stacked up and waiting to land. Smith continued to cajole the heavily pressured air traffic controller at Newark airport to give him landing clearance, based purely on his ability to find his way down the glide path and onto the runway by sight.

A dense and impenetrable fog rolling in from the sea had reduced visibility in the New York area to a mere 220 yards (200m). As the B-25 crossed over New York, Smith apparently became disorientated in the foggy conditions, and office workers in New York's skyscrapers reported watching the hapless aircraft weaving through the towering concrete jungle. Without the benefit of either a cockpit voice recorder or a flight data recorder (both of which were not to be seen on the flight decks of aircraft until the mid 1960s) it is difficult to know how Lt. Col. Smith strayed so perilously from his flight path.

At about 1000 hours the aircraft smashed into the 79th floor of the Empire State Building in New York, a height of some 1000 feet (305m). Wreckage plowed through the building, smashing through solid walls and spreading burning fuel across the floor. One of the engines severed the cable in a lift shaft, sending the lift and its female attendant plummeting 1000 feet (305m) to the basement. Incredibly, she was saved by the giant springs that had been placed in the basement for just such an eventuality.

Burning wreckage from the aircraft crashed on to the street below. Miraculously only 13 people were killed, including the three occupants of the aircraft.

daredevil, who was used to getting his own way. He had over 50 combat missions to his name on B-17 Flying Fortresses, but it was only the second time he had flown a B-25, which was lighter and faster. On this fateful morning Smith was flying without the benefit of a navigator

Smith was scheduled to pick up some fellow army officers at Newark airport, New Jersey, where he had dropped them the previous evening. However, reports of bad weather at Newark meant that most of the aircraft landing at Newark that morning were requesting they be guided in using an instrument approach,

GRAND CANYON, ARIZONA, USA

JUNE 30, 1956

The huge expansion in the popularity of air travel during the 1950s placed a great burden on the limited capacity of US air traffic control. Despite the introduction of professional air traffic controllers in 1929, the system had not kept pace with the increasing distances and greater volumes of human traffic on internal US routes. The United Airlines-TWA collision in June 1956 proved not only the most costly civil air accident in human terms of that decade, but also highlighted the woeful inadequacies of this system.

The Super Constellation (the TWA aircraft involved in the crash) was introduced into service in 1951. The Douglas DC-7 (the United Airlines aircraft) was designed following a request by American Airlines for a commercial competitor on US trunk routes to the TWA Super Constellations.

In the late morning of Saturday, June 30, the TWA Super Constellation took off in fine conditions from Los Angeles International airport, California, on a scheduled service to Kansas, and eventually Washington, DC. It was followed a few minutes later by

Left: The Grand Canyon in Arizona is a spectacular feature. The passengers of the TWA Super Constellation and the United Airlines DC-7 were probably craning to catch a glimpse of the breathtaking view when their aircraft collided, killing all on board.

the two aircraft were set to cross over the Grand Canyon. Once out of the jurisdiction of the Los Angeles air traffic control, the two aircraft were in uncontrolled airspace, and they would be operating under visual flight rules. This meant that it became the sole responsibility of the flight crew to avoid other aircraft in the area. However, the air traffic controller responsible for both flights was at fault for failing to inform either crew of other aircraft movements in the area.

With nothing to warn them of the impending collision, the passengers of the TWA aircraft were probably gazing down through the cloud hoping to catch a glimpse of the spectacular scenery of the Grand Canyon when the collision occurred. The DC-7 was descending – ironically, the DC-7's captain was probably trying to provide his passengers with a better view. The rear fuselage of the Super Constellation was torn off in the impact, which also destroyed the outer section of the port wing on the DC–7.

With no means of controlling the aircraft, the TWA Constellation plummeted almost vertically upside down into the canyon. The DC-7 impacted about a mile away on the steep slopes of the canyon wall. All 58 people on board the DC-7, and all 70 of those on the TWA Constellation were killed.

Above: *An aerial view showing (upper arrow) where the wreck of the DC-7 was found and (bottom arrow) where the Constellation was found.*

Right: *Pieces of the Constellation strewn over the side of the Canyon.*

the United Airlines DC-7, bound for Chicago, Illinois, where it was due to make a stopover before completing the final leg of its journey to Newark, New Jersey.

The faster DC-7 climbed to a cruising altitude that was slightly higher than that of the Super Constellation and both aircraft headed out across the Mojave Desert. Encountering cloud above the desert the pilot of the TWA Constellation requested permission from the Los Angeles air traffic control center to climb to 21,000 feet (6400m), but as the United Airlines DC-7 was flying in the same direction at this height the Constellation's request was denied.

Fatally however, the Constellation's pilot was cleared to fly above the cloud layer – which also meant flying at approximately 21,000 feet (6400m). As they were flying on slightly different headings, the paths of

NEW YORK, USA

DECEMBER 16, 1960

Four years after the collision of a United Air Lines Douglas DC-7 and a TWA Super Constellation over the Grand Canyon, a similar accident occurred over the district of Brooklyn in New York. It involved the same two carriers, virtually identical aircraft, and it cost the same number of lives. It also showed that, despite a program of improvements, US air traffic control procedures were still fraught with problems.

The United Airlines DC-8 was on approach to New York International airport at the end of a scheduled service from Chicago. Weather conditions were poor, with visibility reduced to the extent that the crew were forced to rely on instrument readings to fly the aircraft.

The TWA Lockheed Super Constellation had originated at Dayton, Ohio, and was to land at La Guardia, New York's other major airport. At 1033 hours on December 16, 1960, as the two aircraft were descend-

Below: The tailplane and wing of the crashed Douglas airliner lie in a street in Brooklyn as firemen play their hoses over the wreckage.

Right: The impact of the exploding Douglas DC-8 wraught havoc in the Park Slope area of Brooklyn.

ing toward their separate destinations, they collided in cloud over Miller Army Air Field on Staten Island.

The United Airlines DC-8 crashed into the upper fuselage of the Constellation from behind, causing the latter aircraft to break into three parts and plummet to the ground on Staten Island from a height of 5000 feet (1500m). The crippled DC-8 carried on for another 8.5 miles (13.5km) before impacting in the Park Slope area of Brooklyn.

The resulting explosion caused extensive damage to buildings in the vicinity, and killed six people on the ground. An 11-year-old boy survived the crash of the jetliner but died of his injuries in hospital soon after, joining the list of 134 fatalities.

Left: Pieces of wreckage from the DC-8 are loaded aboard a truck during the clearing up operations following the aircraft's horrific crash into the streets of Brooklyn.

TENERIFE, CANARY ISLANDS

MARCH 27, 1977

As word of this accident spread across the holiday island of Tenerife in the early evening of Sunday, March 27, 1977, local hospitals were inundated with people generously offering their assistance as blood donors. Despite their efforts, and those of the emergency crews who rushed to the scene of carnage at Los Rodeos airport, this infamous disaster remains the world's worst ever commercial air accident. On the runway the inferno caused by the collision of two giant aircraft was still burning two days later. In all 583 people perished, on an island that was no stranger to air tragedy.

Both aircraft, the Royal Dutch Airlines (KLM) Boeing 747 (named *Rhine River*) and the Pan American 747 (named *Clipper Victor*), had been rerouted to Los Rodeos, Tenerife, after a bomb attack at Las Palmas, on the neighbouring island of Gran Canaria, their scheduled destination.

The Dutch aircraft was on a service from Amsterdam, with a complement of 246 passengers and 11 crew members. Commanding the flight was one of KLM's most senior captains, Jacob van Zanten, assisted by First Officer Klass Meurs and Flight Engineer William Schreuder. The PanAm aircraft had originated at Los Angeles, California. During a stopover at New York the crew of nine was changed and a further 103 passengers boarded for the flight to Las Palmas, bringing the total number of passengers to 378. Both aircraft were approaching the end of their flights when the airport at Las Palmas was closed due to the bomb attack. Both crews were told to divert to Tenerife, about 70 miles to the northwest. They landed within 30 minutes of each other early on Sunday afternoon.

It became clear that the airport at Las Palmas was not going to open in the near future, so the Dutch captain disembarked his passengers. He was also aware that the delay could mean his crew would exceed the time limit on their permissible duty hours, and he contacted the KLM operations center at Amsterdam to voice his concerns. The Amsterdam center confirmed that if the crew did not leave Las Palmas for the return flight by 1900 hours that evening they would be in breach of their duty hours limit. Since to do this knowingly would lead to a criminal prosecution, this is something that few experienced pilots would ever risk.

The PanAm *Clipper Victor* touched down at Los Rodeos at 1415 hours but the captain, Victor Grubbs, elected to keep his passengers on board. Because of the increased volume of traffic at Los Rodeos that day, and the normally heavy weekend schedule, aircraft

Above: Of the two jumbo jets involved in this horrific collision on the runway, one was a KLM Boeing 747 like the one shown here.

were parked in any available space. Both the empty *Rhine River* and the *Clipper Victor* were parked just off runway 12 in a designated holding area (an area where taxiing aircraft wait until the crew are cleared for take-off).

Only 15 minutes after the *Clipper Victor* landed, Las Palmas was reopened, and aircraft at Los Rodeos began to leave for the short flight to the neighbouring island. Frustratingly for the crew of *Clipper Victor*, they had been parked behind the Dutch aircraft. Until the passengers had been reembarked the American plane could not take off. Even when this lengthy embarkation process had been completed, news came through of delays at Las Palmas.

The Dutch captain then decided to refuel *Rhine River* at Los Rodeos, in an effort to speed up the turnaround at Las Palmas and stay within his tight schedule. This annoyed the captain of *Clipper Victor*, who had been on duty for over 10 hours by the time this process was completed. As the afternoon wore on the weather at Los Rodeos began to deteriorate, with light rain and fog reducing visibility at times down to 330 yards (300m).

It was almost 1700 hours before both aircraft were ready to depart. Because of the wind direction the crews were requested to taxi from the holding area to the far end of the two-mile (3.2km) long runway. Visibility had deteriorated to a point where it was difficult for the Dutch crew taxiing down the runway to ascertain their position, and for the Spanish tower controller to even see the aircraft. *Rhine River* reached the end of the runway, turned 180°, and radioed to the tower that it was ready for take-off.

The next series of events were undeniably the cause of the tragedy, and can in part be attributed to fatigue, but in the main to human error. Without receiving clearance for take-off, or perhaps because they mistakenly thought they been given it, the flight crew of *Rhine River* began their take-off run.

On the flight deck of *Clipper Victor*, which was still taxiing in the opposite direction down the runway, the crew were anxious to get clear of the runway. The horrified crew then saw the giant Boeing hurtling out of the gloom toward them. Grubbs threw open the throttles and desperately tried to clear out of its path, as the first officer screamed "Get off, get off, get off."

Below: The PanAm 747 in flames after it collided with the KLM 747 while taxiing along the runway in foggy weather.

Right:
Investigators
sifting through
the wreckage after
the worst ever
accident in
commercial
aviation history.

Below: The
charred fuselage
engine and wheel
sections of the
crashed KLM 747.

On the flight deck of the *Rhine River*, the Dutch captain yanked back on the control column, and grounded the tail of his aircraft heavily as he tried to pull up. Despite the actions of both crews, the under-carriage and the outboard engine on the port wing of the Dutch *Rhine River* hit the upper fuselage of the *Clipper Victor*, ripping most of it off. The *Rhine River* flew on for about 500 feet (150m) before sinking back onto the runway. Skidding down the tarmac for another 330 yards (300m), it came to a halt and was immediately engulfed in a huge fireball. Fire crews could do nothing to save any of those on board.

Of those on board the PanAm aircraft, 70 people were pulled from the wreckage, but nine of them succumbed to their injuries in the following weeks, bringing the total terrible death toll to 583.

LOS ANGELES, USA
AUGUST 31, 1986

Recreational flying is extremely popular in southern California, and the pilots of light aircraft passionately defend their right to use the airspace above the state. However, few light aircraft operating out of the numerous airports in the area carry sophisticated avionics equipment and the Piper Archer single engine monoplane involved in this accident was no exception. The transponder it carried was a non-encoding version, which does not register the altitude of the aircraft on the radar screen of an air traffic controller.

In the minutes before this incident, the pilot of the Piper strayed unwittingly into the path of a commercial airliner. Although Los Angeles air traffic control was aware of this intrusion, in the moments before the impact the duty controller's attention was distracted by the appearance on his radar scope of yet another light aircraft that had strayed into the restricted airspace around the terminal.

An Aeromexico McDonnel Douglas DC-9, on the final leg of a scheduled service from Mexico City to Los Angeles, was making its final approach to the runway when it collided with the Piper.

The tailplane of the DC-9 knifed into the the smaller aircraft, killing the pilot and his two passengers – his wife and daughter. The force of the impact tore off part of the Mexican aircraft's tailplane, causing it to roll over and enter a terminal 45° dive.

Falling on a residential area in the Los Angeles suburbs, the Mexican DC-9 airliner exploded in a fireball. All 64 people on board were killed, together with another 15 on the ground. Wreckage from the Piper monoplane crashed down into a schoolyard a few hundred yards (metres) away, but miraculously there were no further casualties.

Right: The scene on the ground after a Mexican DC-9 hit a private monoplane and crashed into a residential area in a Los Angeles suburb, destroying at least 10 houses.

RAMSTEIN, WEST GERMANY

AUGUST 28, 1988

Military aerobatic close formation flying is the ultimate test of skill and nerves, and a fiercely competitive arena in which pilots from the world's air forces try to show each other how good they are. They may also be putting the aircraft through its paces to impress potential customers. In short, they are the very public face of a country's military air forces.

The competition to win one of the coveted places in these teams, such as the British Red Arrows, or the Italian Frecce Tricolori, is intense, and only highly experienced pilots are considered for what many of their colleagues regard as a glamorous posting.

The Italian Air Force's Frecce Tricolori team was nearing the end of its display in front of a huge 100,000

strong crowd of German nationals and US service personnel at the NATO airbase at Ramstein in West Germany when this incident occurred.

At 1535 hours the team was performing a cross-over maneuver when the solo lead pilot, Lt. Col. Ivo Nutallari, collided with the main group as they flew in close formation along the crowd line. Highly inflammable jet fuel and burning wreckage rained down on to the ground and cut a path through the crowd, killing 30 spectators, the three pilots involved in the collision, and injuring at least 60 other spectators. Many people were seriously burned and 13 spectators later died in hospital of their wounds. It was later assessed that the team had transgressed a strict air display rule by flying a maneuver that involved a solo aircraft flying directly at the crowd.

Below: The Frecce Tricolori team of Aermacchi MB 339 were giving a display at the Ramstein air show when they were involved in a fatal collision immediately over the heads of the crowd.

56

CANTON, CHINA

OCTOBER 2, 1990

Above: The wreckage of a Chinese airliner strewn across the runway at Baiyin airport after being struck by the hijacked jetliner.

China has proved a valuable and profitable market for Boeing. This ground collision, following the hijack of one of the planes, involved three aircraft purchased from Boeing – a Xiamen Airlines Boeing Advanced 737, a China Southwest Airlines Boeing 707, and a China Southern Airlines Boeing 757.

Chinese authorities rarely divulge information on air accidents involving the dozen or so air carriers operating out of that country. Even so, China has an exemplary record of air safety, and this tragedy, the most costly in the dark history of air piracy, can be attributed only in small part to ground control procedures at Baiyin airport. The greater part of the guilt lies with the pirate himself. His desperate act cost 132 innocent people their lives.

Xiamen Airlines, one of the newer operators in China, operates regular services on a number of internal routes. A Boeing Advanced 737, one of a fleet of 737 jetliners owned by Xiamen, was making a routine domestic flight between Xiamen, in the province of Fujian, to Canton 230 miles (370km) to the southwest. At an unconfirmed time during the flight, a young man announced to cabin crew members that he had explosives strapped to his body, and demanded that the pilot reroute to Taiwan, where he presumably was seeking political asylum.

The hijacker ordered all the flight crew except the pilot out of the cockpit. The pilot attempted to reason with the young man, informing him (correctly) that the 737 had insufficient fuel reserves for the flight to Taiwan. As a compromise, the captain offered to fly to Hong Kong, but his pleas fell on deaf ears. The aircraft continued on its heading toward Canton, and then began to circle, as the captain tried in vain to convince his hijacker of the futility of his demands.

These negotiations went on for some time, until low fuel warnings began to sound on the flight deck. This left the captain with no choice but to attempt a landing at Baiyin airport, serving Canton.

Moments before touching down, the hijacker appears to have attempted to wrest control of the aircraft, causing it to thump down hard onto the runway and swerve left into a "holding area". Still travelling at considerable speed, the starboard wing of the 737 sliced into the forward fuselage of a parked China Southwest Airlines 707. The pilot, who was on the flight deck performing routine preflight checks, was only slightly injured.

Also standing in the path of the runaway jet was a China Southern Airlines 757, awaiting take-off clearance for a scheduled flight to Shanghai. Colliding with the port wing and upper central fuselage of the 757, the Xiamen 737 turned upside down and finally came to a halt. Of the 104 passengers on board the Xiamen 737, 84 died in the tragedy, along with 47 people on the 757 and the driver of a vehicle.

The Chinese authorities, who are usually reluctant to criticize their own procedures, admitted that it had been a serious mistake to allow an aircraft to taxi while a hijacked aircraft was attempting to land.

CHARKHI DADRI, NEAR NEW DELHI, INDIA

NOVEMBER 12, 1996

Above: Firemen hose down the remains of the Saudi Boeing 747 that collided in mid-air with a Kazakhstan cargo plane on November 12, 1996.

The cargo freighter version of the Ilyushin IL-76 was developed in the late 1960s as an aircraft able to carry 40 tonnes of cargo to the outposts of the Soviet Union, where airstrips were often rough and ready. It entered service in 1975, and when the Soviet Union was dissolved, many former Aeroflot aircraft were transferred to Kazakhstan Airlines.

At about 1830 hours on Tuesday evening, November 12, a Saudi Boeing 747 took off from New Delhi airport

Right: On impact the two colliding aircraft disintegrated in mid-air and the wreckage was distributed over a wide area. Everyone on board the two planes was killed.

Left: Indian policemen stand guard by the debris of the Kazakhstan Ilyushin IL-76 freighter outside the village of Chadkhi Dadri.

bound for Riyadh in Saudi Arabia. Many of the 289 passengers were Indian nationals returning to their jobs in Saudi Arabia. They were served by 23 crew members.

The inbound Kazakhstan Airlines aircraft, an Ilyushin IL-76, was approaching the end of its flight from the central Asian republic of Kazakhstan. On board were 10 crew members, 27 passengers and a considerable payload in cargo.

At 1840 hours, as the Saudi aircraft climbed through 14,000 feet (4200m) to its cruising height, the giant IL-76 collided with it. Both aircraft disintegrated almost instantaneously.

Wreckage was scattered over a wide area near the village of Charkhi Dadri, about 60 miles (96km) west of New Delhi. All those on board both aircraft – 349 people – were killed.

WEATHER

One of the most unpredictable and therefore potentially one of the greatest threats to air safety is the weather. A competent and experienced pilot is usually also a skilled meteorologist, with the ability to assess the potential threat of, for example, a tropical storm system, the effect that a strong headwind will have on his fuel consumption, and the way in which the altitude of the airport may affect the take-off run. In the modern era of air travel the flight crew have the benefit of a range of sophisticated ground and air weather radar systems at their disposal, together with global satellite networks that can provide up-to-the-minute information at any point along the route of their flight.

It is certainly true to say that in the last two decades of the 20th century the application of technologies such as these have helped to reduce the negative influence of poor weather conditions on aircraft operations. However, this was certainly not always the case. There are weather phenomena that for many years were virtually unpredictable. One of the most infamous of these, the so-called microburst, caused two of the disasters described in the following pages. Only recently have scientists begun to understand the phenomenon and accurate and reliable warning systems have now become available.

Ice was the enemy of pioneer aviators, and can still be no less of a hazard in cold climates if proper precautions are not observed. This was proved at least once during the 1970s, when an aircraft flown by a pilot with virtually no experience of cold-weather operations crashed shortly after take-off because the wings were heavy with ice.

Right: Wreckage from the Arrow Air DC-10 that crashed in Newfoundland with ice on its wings in the depths of the Canadian winter of 1985.

ALLONNE, NORTHERN FRANCE

OCTOBER 5, 1930

Much time and considerable amounts of money were invested in an ambitious British airship program in the 1920s. The long distances that airships were capable of flying seemed an ideal means of communicating between the far flung corners of the British empire.

Two airships, the R100 and the R101, were on the drawing board by 1924. The design specifications for the R101, to be built at the Royal Airship works at Cardington, England, called for a machine capable of flying the 3500 or so miles (7240km) to the Indian sub-continent, with a payload of 30 tons made up of passengers, their baggage, and cargo such as mail. The proposed design was a mammoth 724 feet (220m) long, by 63 feet (19m) high.

During the first six years of development the program ran into many teething problems. The gas bags were prone to rub on the rigid frame and split. Coupled with this, the weight of the giant airship far exceeded the parameters set by the design team, forcing them to undergo an extensive program of weight saving. Among other things, two of the lavatories in the passenger car were removed. To increase the lifting capacity an extra 53 feet (16m) was added to the structure, increasing the length to 777 feet (236m).

By the time the R101 was anchored at its mast at Cardington for the maiden voyage to India in September 1930 the program was well over schedule and hugely over budget. The ever eager British press, and the Secretary of State for Air Lord Cardington, continued to herald the airship as a triumph of British aviation. It was certainly an imposing sight, and given the ambitious specifications that the technical staff were given to work with, a triumph over many adversities. But the R101 was never tested adequately. Just one test had been deemed necessary before the airship was ready for the flight to India. This test flight had been conducted in near-perfect weather conditions.

Fifty-four people boarded the R101 in the early evening of October 4, 1930, including many high ranking Air Ministry officials and the leading figures in the airship development program. Incredibly, the airship was awarded its Certificate of Airworthiness only minutes before take-off. At 1900 hours the giant airship rose into the air and set a southeast course for Paris, France.

Problems arose almost immediately with one of the engines, which was shut down. At barely 40mph (64km/h) the R101 flew over London, and three hours after departing from Cardington crossed the English

coast near Hastings. By now the weather had deteriorated considerably and the airship was being buffeted by high winds. As it began drifting eastwards off its course to Paris, engineers realized that rain soaking into the outer skin had also added nearly three tons in weight to the airship.

At just a few minutes past 0200 hours on October 5, as the airship struggled to make headway against a

Above: The burnt out skeleton of the R101 airship lying on the side of Beauvais Ridge near the village of Allonne in northern France.

Above: *Rescue workers remove a body from the scene of the R101 crash.*

Left: *After the inferno that consumed the R101 airship, little remained but the rigid frame.*

strong headwind, the outer skin on the nose was torn. Soon after, the two forward gas bags were ruptured, and as gas rushed through the gaping tears, the nose of the R101 pitched down. At this point the watch commander sealed the fate of many of those on board by ordering the engine power to be reduced. This action cancelled out any aerodynamic lift generated by forward motion of the airship, which might have allowed the airship to continue flying.

The R101 struck the side of the Beauvais Ridge near the village of Allonne at 0209 hours. Fire broke out in the control car directly under the main gas bags, and in seconds the inferno had swamped the whole machine. Four of the engineers and a wireless operator managed to scramble clear.

The loss of the R101 led directly to the cancellation of the airship program in Britain, although the German nation championed this type of flying machine for another six years.

ATLANTIC OCEAN, OFF NEW JERSEY, USA

APRIL 4, 1933

The USS airship *Akron* and her sister ship *Macon* were designed to carry fighter planes in a docking bay and hangar. These planes, it was thought, could both provide protection for the airship and scout for enemy forces. Aircraft were still hampered by limited range and an airship aircraft carrier would provide the ultimate mobile base on the new, modern battlefield.

The *Akron* had less structural bracing than most German airships, and another major difference was that the *Akron* had internally mounted engines. The airship was filled with nonflammable helium, which meant that the power plants could be mounted inter-

nally for ease of maintenance and improved streamlining. The *Akron*'s eight props were built on outriggers on either side of the ship.

On April 3, 1933, the *Akron*, under the command of Commander Frank McCord, was flying off the coast of New Jersey, fighting its way through a thunderstorm. Also on board were Rear Admiral William Moffett, chief of the Navy Bureau of Aeronautics, and Commander Frederick Berry, commander of the Lakehurst Naval Air Station. The storm that the *Akron* was flying through was one of the worst that the New Jersey coast had seen in years. Because of the winds, heavy cloud cover, and ground fog the navigator was unable to determine their position. The captain

Left: The Akron *was a US naval airship designed as an aircraft carrier that could transport fighter planes long distances to where they were needed.*

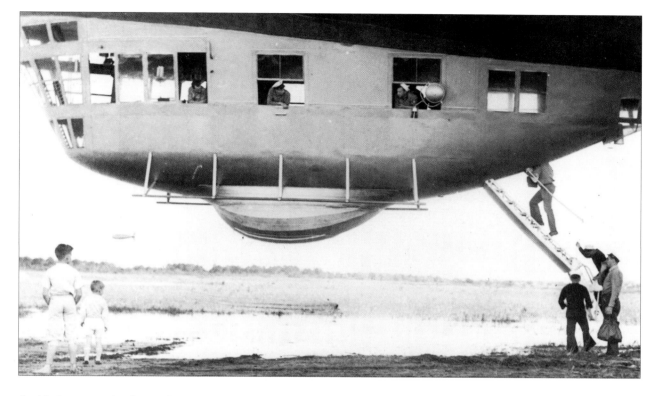

Right: US naval personnel boarding the Akron *at a naval air base in the year before the disaster.*

decided to turn back to shore but failed to locate a break in the storm. The order was given to head back out to sea and simply ride out the weather. Eventually the *Akron* found some calm air.

At 0015 hours the *Akron* was rocked by a horrific blow. The calm that the unfortunate airship had felt was in fact the eye of the storm system. As it emerged from the other side of the eye, fierce winds caused the massive airship to buck wildly. The ship hit an enormous downdraft and was sucked down almost 1000 feet (300m). Only by dropping most of the water ballast and bringing the engines to full power could the descent be stopped.

The *Akron* was able to gain altitude briefly, but was pushed down again and again until finally the force of the storm started to rip the ship apart. With loss of control of the fins the *Akron* smashed into the freezing water of the Atlantic.

Because the *Akron* carried no life vests and there had not been enough time to lower her one life raft, 72 of her 76-man crew drowned, including Rear Admiral Moffett along with Commanders Berry and McCord.

Below: The wreck of the Akron *adrift in the storm-tossed seas off New Jersey.*

MUNICH AIRPORT, WEST GERMANY

FEBRUARY 6, 1958

This disaster achieved instant global notoriety, mainly because of the aircraft's prized passengers, the Manchester United Football Club's "Busby Babes" – a young and dynamic side that had just qualified for the semi-finals of the European Cup Championship in Belgrade, and was now returning home to Manchester via Munich.

The sunshine of Belgrade gave way to icy rain and snow as the British European Airways Airspeed Ambassador 2 closed in on Munich. As the aircraft descended through 18,000 feet (5400m) of cloud, the pilot activated the airframe anti-icing system, which heated the tail plane, fins, and wings to 60 degrees Celsius. Landing was normal except that huge plumes of slush sprayed up from the nose wheel. This would later prove to be critical.

A thick layer of slush enveloped Munich's runways that day, but at that time virtually nothing was known of the drag effects of a contaminated runway. The slush had now been measured at half an inch (1cm) on the busiest points of the runway, but its depth at the runway's end was still unknown.

After re-fuelling the pilots inspected the wings of the aircraft for ice and snow. Ice or snow on an aircraft's upper surfaces affects lift by impeding the airflow, but as there was only a slight film of ice that was thawing and running clear, the pilots deemed de-icing to be unnecessary. Later this became the basis for the authorities' charge of pilot negligence.

As the aircraft accelerated for take-off the co-pilot (flying as pilot) suddenly shouted "abandon take-off". The reason was "boost surging", caused by an over-rich fuel mixture, which was compounded by the thin air at Munich's high altitude.

After another abandoned take-off, this time due to a loss of power in one engine, the pilots conferred with the station engineer. One option was to re-tune the engines, but this was rejected since it would take all night. They decided upon one last attempt, this time releasing the throttles as slowly as possible.

However, when the flight crew eased off on the throttles to deal with the surging they found that they needed more runway to become airborne. The slush that was causing the trouble was at its deepest at precisely the point where the aircraft needed to achieve maximum acceleration.

With the nose wheel off the ground, and great plumes of slush rushing past the passenger windows, the flight crew committed themselves to take-off. But

Above: A BEA Airspeed Ambassador aircraft similar to the one that crashed at Munich.

Right: Rescue attempts at the scene of the crash were hampered by the icy rain and snow that enveloped the airport.

Below: A week after the crash salvage operators remove pieces of wreckage of the aircraft for investigation.

the aircraft never managed to reach the minimum speed required to become airborne. As the aircraft approached the end section of the runway, all the flight crew could do was watch as their speed plummeted. They ran out of runway well short of the speed needed to lift them off it.

The aircraft plowed through the snow beyond the runway, smashed through a wooden fence, and then squared up to a house and a tree across the road. In desperation the flight crew raised the undercarriage in an attempt to get airborne. But the left wing and the tail struck the house, and the tree tore apart the cockpit. Just 100 yards (90m) past the house the aircraft hit a wooden hut which sheared off the complete tail section. The remaining forward section catapulted across the snow for another 70 yards (64m) before coming to rest in a field.

Of the 44 people on board, 23 died, including eight "Busby Babes", four Manchester United staff, eight journalists covering the big match, a Yugoslav passenger, an air steward, and the co-pilot. The pilot survived, and after a decade of disputes between him and the German authorities, the drag effects of slush on take-off were finally properly tested and recognized. However, ice on the wings remained the official cause of the accident.

MOUNT FUJIAMA, JAPAN

MARCH 5, 1966

Prior to this incident, British Overseas Airways Corporation (BOAC) had suffered no fatal air accidents during the 1960s, an admirable record considering the vast increase in the volume of passengers carried by the airline. This record was broken tragically on March 5, 1966. It was on this date that a Boeing 707 operated by the company was torn apart in the air by violent turbulence at an altitude of 15,000 feet (5000m), near the towering summit of Mount Fujiama in Japan.

Captain Bernard Dobson had taken off from Haneda airport (serving Tokyo) for the 1100-mile (1800-km) leg to Hong Kong, which was part of a scheduled round-the-world service that had left London four days previously. In order to give his (mostly American) passengers a view of the mountain, he deviated from the designated airway and flew west.

Fifty miles (80km) south west of Tokyo, the aircraft flew into severe turbulence. Buffeted by gusts of wind, it began to disintegrate. Parts of the aircraft were detached and fell off. The rear control surfaces and the rear fuselage were torn off and the stricken jetliner began to tumble out of the sky. As it fell, the fuselage and main engine assemblies were ripped off.

Pieces of wreckage and the bodies of all 124 people on board were recovered from a wide area at the foot of the mountain.

This crash shook the aviation community, more particularly as it occurred less than 24 hours after the crash of a Canadian Pacific DC-8 at Haneda, with the loss of 64 lives.

Below: Japanese soldiers searching for bodies in the wreckage of the crashed BOAC Boeing 707.

NEW YORK, USA

JUNE 24, 1975

Dark skies gathered over John F. Kennedy airport in the late afternoon of July 24, 1975. A menacing thunderstorm brought pounding rain, violent and unpredictable winds, and precisely the kind of conditions in which the weather phenomenon known as a microburst can occur.

The crash of the Eastern Airlines Boeing 727 was one of three incidents that occurred in the United States within a decade of each other that were attributed to wind shear associated with microbursts. In a microburst a downward moving column of air can cause an aircraft to drop suddenly, sometimes with fatal results.

On the afternoon of July 24, Eastern Airlines Flight 66 was on a scheduled service from New Orleans, Louisiana. After they had contacted approach controllers at JFK, the flight crew were requested to land the aircraft on Runway 22. The pilots of two aircraft who had landed on this same runway only minutes previously had reported experiencing very strong wind shear. One reported nearly crashing. Despite this fact the tower controller did not consider it necessary to close the runway.

The Eastern Airlines Boeing 727 was about 1.2 miles (1.9km) from the end of the runway when it was suddenly lifted by an updraught of air. Without warning, this suddenly changed to a down draught, and the supporting headwind dropped away. This caused the aircraft to descend rapidly, with the down draught continuing to increase.

Still more than three quarters of a mile (1.2km) from the end of the runway, the 727 struck a row of tall approach-light gantries, one of which tore off the outer tip of the port wing. Plowing through more of the unyielding metal towers, the aircraft was virtually demolished before it even hit the ground, scattering flaming wreckage across a road barely 260 feet (80m) from the end of the runway. Of the people on board 109 passengers and six crew members perished; seven passengers and two stewardesses survived, all with serious injuries.

Left: Rescue workers sifting through the debris of the Eastern Airlines Boeing 727 crash on June 24, 1975, in which 115 people died.

WASHINGTON, USA

JANUARY 13, 1982

On a bitterly cold January afternoon, in the depths of one of the worst American winters on record, 78 people died when the Air Florida Boeing 727 that was carrying them to the warmer climes of Fort Lauderdale and Tampa, in Florida, smashed into a bridge and plunged into the ice-covered waters of the Potomac River.

Only the tail of the aircraft remained above the surface, and four passengers and a stewardess who had been seated in the rear of the cabin were able to scramble free and cling to the wreckage. A Bell LongRanger helicopter of the US Park Police arrived on the scene within 20 minutes, and plucked them from the freezing water. Two pedestrians on the bridge bravely dived into the water to assist in a desperate search for survivors. One of them undoubtedly saved the life of a woman who had lapsed into unconsciousness and lost her grip on a rescue line.

It was later concluded that one of the primary factors in the crash was the presence of ice on the wings and in the engine intakes. Although the 727 had been de-iced (common procedure in cold weather aircraft operations) about 60 minutes before the accident, this allowed sufficient time for ice to build up on the wings again. This in turn seriously hampered the performance of the aircraft when it became airborne, and caused it to enter an unrecoverable stall.

Below: The Boeing 727 had just taken off from Washington National Airport when it crashed into a road bridge. Here rescue workers on the bank of the partly frozen Potomac River help survivors ashore.

NEW ORLEANS, USA

JULY 9, 1982

Right: A Pan American Boeing 727 similar to the one that crashed after taking off from Moisant International Airport, New Orleans, on July 9, 1982.

The term "microburst" is probably unfamiliar to most of the millions of people who board commercial airliners every year, but it is a word that strikes fear into the hearts of many an experienced pilot. It is a weather phenomenon – most often found in stormy conditions – in which a column of air moves rapidly downward and mushrooms out in all directions on reaching the ground. An aircraft flying into a microburst can experience a rapid loss in altitude, and often there is little or nothing the crew can do to recover.

For many years the microburst was a completely unexplained phenomenon. The accident described here prompted an extensive investigation into microburst that led to the development of low level wind shear alert systems (LLWAS). Although not foolproof, these could help to prevent a repetition of similar incidents.

Most modern airports are now fitted with LLWAS that can detect the presence of microbursts. This equipment is positioned at the ends of runways, to provide air traffic controllers with information they can relay to any aircraft preparing to take off or land. Unfortunately, at the time when this incident occurred, the technology was very much in its infancy.

The southern United States are prone to sudden and spectacular summer thunderstorms, which rise over the Gulf of Mexico before sweeping along across the Mississippi Delta. Just such a storm blew in to the New Orleans area on the afternoon of July 9, 1982. At Moisant International Airport, serving New Orleans, Pan American Flight 759 – a Boeing 727 – was being prepared for the second leg of a three-leg scheduled service from Miami, Florida, to San Diego, California.

With preparations completed, and the passengers embarked, the crew taxied to the end of Runway 10 in anticipation of take-off. It was raining heavily at the time, the cloud base was at around 4000 feet (1200m), and visibility was approaching 2 miles (3km).

The captain had plenty of experience in such conditions and had been warned by airport meteorological staff of the likelihood of wind shear only five minutes before he was cleared for take-off. The crew of the 727 also tried to predict the weather conditions they would encounter in their immediate flight path by viewing the

Left: The wreckage of the PanAm 727 litters the ground around a house that caught fire after the aircraft crashed into a residential neighbourhood, killing eight people on the ground.

aircraft's weather radar, but the heavy rain probably prevented them from observing the threatening storm cells (which could have given rise to a microburst) in their path.

Moments after take-off, the Boeing 727 flew into a microburst that tossed it about the sky. The first officer, who was piloting the aircraft, battled helplessly and in vain to arrest the airliner's descent. After striking a stand of trees 2400 feet (730m) from the end of the runway the 727 impacted the ground and disintegrated. All 153 people on board were killed, as well as eight people on the ground.

The inquiry could find no fault in the operating procedures of either the airline or the flight crew.

Above: Rescue workers survey the scene of devastation created by the crashed Boeing 727.

NEWFOUNDLAND, CANADA

DECEMBER 12, 1985

Right: The wreck of the Arrow Air DC-8 lies on a wooded hillside after crashing half a mile from Gander International Airport.

ce always spells trouble for aircraft. Even a very thin sheet over the lifting and control surface can be potentially hazardous. In this case, it may have been the cause of a tragic crash.

Almost all of the passengers on the Arrow Air DC-8 scheduled flight of December 12, 1985, were US soldiers returning home to Kentucky after service in the Middle East.

After taking off from Cairo airport, the jetliner flew to Gander International Airport in Newfoundland, which was in the depths of a Canadian winter. Sleet probably started to accumulate on the wings of the DC-8 during the stopover, and then froze onto the leading edge and upper surfaces of the wings. The DC-8 was already heavily burdened with the troops and their equipment; and reports subsequently showed that the crew had in fact underestimated the necessary take-off speed and "nose-up" angle required for the weight of the aircraft.

The DC-8 took off in the predawn darkness at 0645 hours, struggled to a height of only 120 feet (40m), and then began – ominously – to descend. Early morning commuters on the Trans-Canada highway were stunned to see the stricken aircraft pass only a few feet over their cars, before crashing into a wooded hillside barely half a mile from the end of the runway. Flames engulfed the aircraft, killing everyone on board.

The board of inquiry was unable to reach any firm conclusions as to the cause of the crash.

MECHANICAL FAILURE

By far the largest number of air crashes are attributable to structural or systems failures. However technologically advanced an aircraft may be, it is only as reliable as the technician who assembles or maintains it. In a machine made up of hundreds of thousands of individual components, even the most rigorous testing and approval procedures can overlook a fault – a faulty rivet, a hairline crack – that could over a period of time develop into a major problem.

Many of the commercial aircraft in service today annually clock up millions of miles in the process of ferrying people across the globe. Some were constructed as long ago as the 1960s, but all are subjected to minute scrutiny, and if necessary rigorous rebuilding programs, to ensure their reliability. Even so, initial design faults, faulty servicing, and metal fatigue can compromise the safe and efficient operation of an aircraft, and ultimately lead to tragic accidents. Analysing these incidents forms a vital part of the process of improving aircraft safety.

No cost-effective aircraft can be designed to withstand every conceivable hazard, and in the end it comes down to money – balancing risk against the maximum cost that the traveling public will pay for the convenience of flying from A to B.

Right: A corroded connecting pin led to the loss of an engine of a Boeing 747 freighter aircraft, which then crashed into an apartment house in Amsterdam, destroying much of the building and killing 47 residents.

LAKEHURST, NEW JERSEY, USA

MAY 6, 1937

There are few more arresting images of the 20th century than that of the Zeppelin *Hindenburg*, its aft quarters engulfed in a ball of flame, lighting the night sky above Lakehurst, New Jersey. The *Hindenburg* was the largest of the many rigid airships – dirigibles – built in Germany between 1900 and 1940, and is still the largest such craft ever constructed. Its loss was a great blow to the prestige of the German airship industry and its manufacturer, Luftschiffbau Zeppelin (LZ). Confidence in the airship was never fully restored after the disaster.

The *Hindenburg* was the last but one in the LZ series (*luftschiff* means airship), and a direct descendant of the Zeppelins that had struck awe and terror into the hearts of Londoners during World War I. The airship had proved too vulnerable as an offensive bombing platform during that conflict, and so the numerous airship manufacturers in Europe and America had begun to look for alternative applications for the technology.

Luftschiffbau Zeppelin, the company established by Ferdinand Graf von Zeppelin in 1900, seemed the most likely to succeed. The 100-hour flights that were a regular feature of the Zeppelin raids on England made

Below: The Hindenburg *sails over New York, en route to Lakehurst, New Jersey, after a transatlantic flight from Germany in 1936. On the left is the Empire State building.*

Above: The newly-completed airship Hindenburg *emerging from its shed for the first time.*

circumnavigation of the globe in 21 days. When the *Graf Zeppelin* was finally decommissioned in early 1937, the future of the airship seemed bright.

The *Hindenburg*, the airship built to supersede the *Graf Zeppelin*, was a truly awe-inspiring sight. Designed by Dr Hugo Eckener, the foremost airship expert of the day, the airship measured 804 feet (245m) from tip to stern. It was powered by four 1,100hp diesel engines located in streamlined nacelles attached at points on the side of the light, but strong, duraluminum rigid frame. The gas cells that provided the lifting power were filled with volatile hydrogen – a lighter-than-air gas.

Eckener's original intention was to fill the cells with nonflammable helium. Unfortunately for the Germans about 90 percent of the world's supplies of helium at this time were produced in a small area of Texas. With an airship program of its own the US Congress was unwilling to allow the expensive gas to be exported.

The presence of huge quantities of a highly inflammable gas, some have argued, made the *Hindenburg* little more than an accident waiting to happen – a flying bomb. The design team were certainly aware of the dangers; the gas bags were brushed with a gelatin solution to prevent gas escaping, and both passengers and crew had to observe rigorous safety procedures. The men patrolling the walkways wore hemp-soled shoes (to prevent any chance sparks from boot nails) and anti-static overalls. In the smoking room, a steward stood watch night and day and the walls were

transatlantic flight a realistic possibility. Such performances, far in excess of anything attainable by conventional fixed-wing aircraft at the time, encouraged the company to experiment with commercial passenger carrying airships, and in September 1928 LZ inaugurated a transatlantic service with the *Graf Zeppelin*. This airship completed 590 flights, 144 of them across the North Atlantic, for a total of more than 1,000,000 miles (1,600,000km). In 1929 the airship made a

Right: The last moments of the Hindenburg, *as it bursts into flames close to its mooring mast at Lakehurst airport, New Jersey.*

Right: The Hindenburg *was filled with highly combustible hydrogen gas – so the slightest spark would turn it into a fireball, as did indeed happen at Lakehurst.*

lined with pigskin to further prevent the risk of fire. Passengers and their luggage were searched for potentially incendiary materials before boarding.

The interior of the airship was splendidly fitted out in the fashion of the luxurious ocean liners of the day – which many thought the airship would eventually replace. Sumptuous velvet upholstery and walnut coachwork graced the passenger suites and dining salon, and in the fully-equipped kitchen, staff prepared elaborate meals for the complement of up to 50 well-heeled passengers. There was even a grand piano, albeit one fashioned from duraluminum and weighing only 112lb (50kg). The airship was the Concorde of its day – a luxury transatlantic ferry and a potent symbol of the technological advancement of Germany under the Third Reich.

The *Hindenburg* made its maiden flight in April 1936, and during the course of the following 12 months the airship made 10 successful and highly publicized transatlantic crossings.

At 2000 hours on May 3, 1937, Captain Max Pruss, the veteran of 16 transatlantic crossings in the *Graf Zeppelin*, gave the order "Up ship," and the *Hindenburg* rose into the air for the first flight to America of the year. At sunrise on May 4 the Hindenburg was passing south of Ireland, heading toward the coast of Newfoundland. The following day the airship ran into headwinds and Pruss was forced to radio ahead to Lakehurst that he expected his landing to be delayed by 12 hours, until 1800 hours on May 6.

The airship flew over Boston and descended to 600 feet (180m) to give the admiring crowd below a good view of the pride of the Zeppelin company. The airship then proceeded down the coast and over the New York skyline. Pruss delayed his approach to the mooring mast at Lakehurst until 1900 hours because of reports of bad weather, but at 1900 the crew were finally given the order to prepare for landing. Gas was vented off, and the landing wheels were released.

At 1921 hours, the lines that would be used to winch the craft down had just been released, when an explosion ripped through the No. 4 gas cell just in front of the fin. In seconds the whole of the after part of the ship was engulfed in a huge fireball, and burning wreckage began falling on the ground crew below. The *Hindenburg* lurched and the tail began to sink to the ground. Passengers leapt for their lives from the control gondola and the crew quarters, and in only 30 seconds the giant airship lay in a smoking ruin on the ground. Remarkably, 62 out of the 97 people on board escaped with their lives, including 23 of the 36 passengers.

Many explanations were forthcoming during the months of investigation by the US Navy and the German government. One suggestion was that the explosion was caused by a device planted by one of the riggers as a demonstration against the Nazi government. A rather more likely explanation was that gas which had escaped from a ruptured gas bag was ignited by the static electricity that had built up in the air during that stormy New York night.

No final conclusion was ever reached as to what had caused the explosion that destroyed the *Hindenburg*. One thing was certain, however. The disaster was a death blow for the airship industry.

WEST BENGAL, INDIA

MAY 2, 1953

Above: A BOAC Comet 1 similar to the aircraft that crashed soon after take-off from Calcutta on May 2, 1953. The airliner was powered by four De Havilland Ghost engines, and carried a flight crew of four, plus two cabin crew, with accommodation for about 40 passengers.

This accident was the third in a series of seven mysterious accidents involving a De Havilland Comet aircraft in the space of 18 months. In April of 1954, all Comets in service were grounded, due to serious questions about the structural integrity of the aircraft.

On the first anniversary of the inauguration of commercial jetliner flights, a Comet 1 in the service of British Overseas Airways Corporation (BOAC) took off from Singapore on a westbound scheduled service to London Heathrow. Captaining the aircraft was one of the more experienced jet pilots in the service of BOAC. Only two months previously a brand-new Comet had been written off at Karachi by a pilot with little or no experience on the type.

Captain Haddon was rather more capable, and handled the take-off (notoriously difficult to judge accurately on the Comet) with precision. The Comet completed the first leg to Calcutta without incident. At Calcutta passengers for Delhi and London – the second and final destinations of the service – were taken on

board. It was just before 1630 hours when the Comet took off from Dum Dum airport at Calcutta. The flight crew began to climb to their cruising height for the transit to Delhi, 800 miles (1287km) to the northwest. Outside, a violent tropical thunderstorm was raging.

Six minutes after take-off, as the Comet was ascending through 10,000 feet (3000m), the aircraft broke up in the air. The wingless Comet plummeted to the ground in flames and exploded in a forest near the village of Jugalgari, some 30 miles (48km) north-west of Calcutta. All 37 passengers and six crew members were killed.

An extensive investigation was immediately launched, both by the Indian government and at the Royal Aircraft Establishment (RAE) at Farnborough, England. Powerful winds had carried wreckage over a large area, and it took many months before an accurate analysis of the incident could be made.

The Indian inquiry concluded that the strength of the turbulence had placed loads on the airframe of the Comet in excess of those which it had been designed to withstand, and of a strength that would have caused

Above: The wreckage of the crashed Comet strewn over the ground near the village of Jugalgari, north-west of Calcutta.

the disintegration of any commercial transport aircraft. There were, however, indications that metal fatigue could have played a role in the accident. However, it proved impossible to substantiate these claims, because the Indian authorities mistakenly disposed of much of the wreckage before the RAE could examine it.

The British inquiry focused on the likelihood that the airframe had been fatally overstressed as Captain Haddon tried to pull out of the dive that the Comet entered when a spar in the port elevator snapped. The British Air Registration Board, who at that time

granted certification to any new British aircraft types, called for more tests to establish susceptibility of the Comet airframe to metal fatigue.

During the following six months a Comet aircraft was subjected to extensive fatigue loading tests that failed to show any evidence that the aircraft was liable to failures.

However, the number of incidents involving the Comet during those crucial early years of its operational life did serious damage to potential export sales and led to the cancellation of many orders.

PARIS, FRANCE

MARCH 3, 1974

Below: French rescue workers and police sort through wreckage of the DC-10 that crashed into a forest near Paris.

In the early 1970s the McDonnell Douglas DC-10 was rapidly acquiring a reputation for being an unlucky aircraft. This accident involving a Turkish Airlines DC-10 resulted in the death of all 346 on board. It was directly attributable to a design fault that had already caused two earlier incidents in which – miraculously – there had been no fatalities.

The rear cargo door of the DC-10 was designed to open outwards, and this meant that when the aircraft was at altitude and the cabin was pressurized, the rear door was being pushed outwards. In June 1972, the door of an American Airlines DC-10 had blown open, but the captain managed to land the aircraft safely. Following this accident, the US Federal Aviation Administration

prepared to issue an order that alterations should be made to the door locks. But for a variety of reasons, and even though the manufacturer was aware of the potentially catastrophic results if the door locks failed at altitude, the order was downgraded to a request that modifications be made.

Two years after the incident involving the American Airlines DC-10, a similar aircraft operated by Turkish Airlines took off at 1230 hours on Sunday, March 3, 1974, from Orly airport, serving Paris, bound for London Heathrow. The aircraft was filled almost to capacity, mostly with British tourists. As the aircraft climbed through 11,000 feet (3300m) over the village of Saint-Pathus, the rear cargo door failed. The aircraft suffered an explosive decompression, entered a steep dive, and impacted at nearly 500mph (800km/h) into a forest. There were no survivors.

Above: Part of the fuselage of the Turkish Airlines DC-10 that crashed in the Forest of Ermenonville shortly after take-off from Orly airport.

Right: Rescuers carry away a body from the crashed aircraft. There were no survivors.

O'HARE AIRPORT, CHICAGO, USA

MAY 25, 1979

Until the Lockerbie disaster in December 1988, this crash of an American Airlines McDonnell Douglas DC-10 was the worst accident involving a US carrier. The incident did nothing to enhance the reputation of the DC-10, and led to the suspension of its certificate of airworthiness by the Federal Aviation Authority.

The story of the disaster reads like a catalog of errors, beginning in the McDonnell Douglas plant, carrying on through the service life of the aircraft, and ending in a fireball one May afternoon with the loss of 273 lives.

The American Airlines DC-10, designated Flight 191, was due to fly a scheduled service between Chicago O'Hare and Los Angeles International airport. After the embarkation of the passengers and preflight checks were completed, the aircraft taxied to Runway 32 and at 1502 hours began rolling. At about 160mph (257km/h) the officer who was operating the radio called "vee-one" – denoting the point at which the DC-10 was committed to take-off. Two seconds before lift-off, the aircraft shuddered violently, and the port engine seemed to lose power.

Observers on the ground saw smoke pouring from the left wing. Unknown to the flight crew, the port engine had detached completely and ripped a large section of the leading edge away, together with vital hydraulic and electrical lines. The flight crew – unaware that the engine had fallen off – carried out standard procedure for engine failure. The first officer pulled back on the control column, lifted off the runway, and proceeded to climb.

Because of the failure of many of the generator systems, the crew still had no indication of the seriousness of their predicament. About 20 seconds after lift-off, at an altitude of less than 300 feet (100m), the left wing suddenly stalled (due to the fact that the lifting slats had retracted because of the loss of hydraulioc

Right: *Debris from the American Airlines DC-10 scattered over the trailer park where it plunged into the ground.*

Above: Federal Aviation authority officials inspect the wreckage of the DC-10 the day after the crash.

Above: Firemen probe through the debris of the crashed DC-10.

power). As the nose dropped below the horizon, the first officer sought in vain to wrest the jetliner from its dive toward the ground.

Thirty-one seconds after lift-off, the aircraft plunged into the ground near a trailer park, instantaneously killing all those on board, as well as two people on the ground. Examination of the wreckage, and of the engine that had been thrown onto the side of the runway, revealed severe cracking.

All DC-10 aircraft in operation were grounded and subjected to careful inspection. Ten of them also revealed fatigue cracking in the wing engine mounts. The damage had been caused by hasty servicing procedures carried out at a number of airlines when the engines were removed from the aircraft for overhaul. At that time, airlines were constantly searching for ways to reduce servicing man hours.

Serious though the loss of an engine was, such an incident had occurred before with the successful recovery of the aircraft involved. However, the main contributing factors to the crash were the retraction of the leading edge slats, which provide essential lift during the early stages of the flight, and the fact that the flight crew decided to reduce power to achieve optimum climb speed. If they had maintained speed, and if the slats had locked mechanically, the accident might well have been averted.

MOUNT OSUTAKA, JAPAN

AUGUST 12, 1985

The crash of the Japan Airlines Boeing 747 into Mount Osutaka on August 12, 1986, was one of the most harrowing, as well as one of the worst, air disasters on record.

Japan Airlines Flight 123 was on a scheduled service from Haneda International Airport, serving Tokyo, to Osaka 250 miles (402km) to the west. Many of the passengers were returning home to be with their families for the traditional festival of Bon. The routine flight would normally have taken a little under an hour.

After taking off at 1812 hours, the Boeing 747 had levelled off to its cruising height of 24,000 feet (7300m) when a loud explosion was heard at the rear of the aircraft. Pressure then began to drop rapidly in the passenger cabin and the emergency oxygen masks dropped from the roof.

As the captain made a Mayday signal to Tokyo Control, one of the cabin crew reported that part of the aft fuselage was missing. The control wires to the rear control surfaces in the 747 run along this section of the fuselage and when the flight crew tried to maneuver the aircraft they found that the controls had been rendered useless. The giant aircraft began to turn ominously northward toward the snow capped peak of Mount Fujiama.

Although the controls had been irrevocably damaged, the flight crew were able to use engine power to steer the aircraft, and despite the total loss of hydraulic power they managed to lower the undercarriage using the back-up system. At about 1844 hours the jumbo began to descend, and after circling perilously over the city of Otsuki righted itself and flew on toward the mountainous region around Takasaki. Despite the considerable efforts of the crew the aircraft crashed at an altitude of about 4800 feet (1463m) into the side of Mount Osutaka.

Rescue crews did not reach the remote mountainous region until 0900 hours the next morning, and found a scene of almost complete devastation. A stewardess, a 12-year-old boy, an eight-year-old girl, and her mother were the only survivors.

Left: A scene of appalling devastation greeted the members of the Japanese Self Defence forces who began a search of the area using a helicopter on the day following the crash.

MANCHESTER INTERNATIONAL AIRPORT, ENGLAND

AUGUST 22, 1985

The year 1985 was particularly costly in human terms for commercial air carriers. Six major incidents during those 12 months cost over 1300 people their lives. One of the most horrific of these incidents was the loss of the British Airtours Boeing Advanced 737 at Manchester International Airport.

The Greek islands enjoyed a significant increase in tourist traffic during the 1980s, and British Airtours, a subsidiary of British Airways, carried many hundreds of thousands of these tourists from Britain. In the early morning of August 22, 1985, a full complement of 130 passengers, and two infants in arms, boarded a British Airtours 737 at Manchester, bound for a vacation on the Greek island of Corfu.

While the passengers stowed overhead baggage, the cabin crew prepared for a busy flight. On the flight deck, preflight checks passed routinely, and the aircraft proceeded to the holding area just off Runway 24. Cleared for take-off, the captain released the brakes and the aircraft began to accelerate smoothly down the centerline. As the 737 speeded through 140mph (225km/h), the flight crew heard a loud thump. Believing that a tire had failed they immediately aborted the take-off run, and informed the control tower of their predicament.

However, what the flight crew had heard was the port engine partially disintegrating. Parts of the engine casing ruptured the fuel tank next to the engine, and as the aircraft began its emergency deceleration, aviation fuel gushed over the red-hot powerplant and ignited.

Left: Police and firemen inspecting the wreck of the British Airtours Boeing 737 which lost an engine and burst into flames during take-off at Manchester airport.

Above: Despite the efforts of the rescue services, 55 people lost their lives in the fire that engulfed the aircraft.

Right: Aviation inspectors check the port engine of the crashed 737.

This fire was not immediately indicated on the flight deck, where the crew were still under the illusion that a tire had burst. The flight crew then used the power of the engine reversers to arrest the progress of the jetliner, which served literally to fan the flames. When the aircraft finally turned off the runway and ground to a halt, the blaze was already intense. Aviation fuel spilled out of the wing tank and formed a flaming lake on the concrete. To further hamper the evacuation, the prevailing wind then fanned the flames toward the aircraft, burning into the passenger cabin within half a minute.

The scene inside the aircraft was chaotic, and as dark clouds of toxic smoke billowed into the cabin, the crew lost precious seconds struggling with a jammed door. Many people were overcome by smoke inhalation as they struggled in the dark and confusion toward emergency exits, and bodies jammed the narrow aisle. The sheer number of passengers, and the fact that two of the exits were engulfed in flames, further hampered the evacuation. Only about 60 seconds after the aircraft ground to a halt, the rear fuselage collapsed. Although the emergency services arrived on the scene with commendable speed, they were unfortunately unable to save 55 of the passengers, almost all of them in the rear cabin. Dozens of the survivors suffered injuries, many of them serious.

The report of the British Air Accident Investigation Branch revealed that the compression chamber of the Pratt and Witney turbofan had cracked and then partially disintegrated due to thermal fatigue. This is caused by continual heating and cooling of metal parts. The engine fitted to the British Airtours aircraft had previously been repaired for a crack in the same area, but the repair was of poor quality.

MARAVATIO, MEXICO

MARCH 31, 1986

One only has to observe an airliner landing to understand the brutal treatment that the main undercarriage is subjected to. Tires are also subject to great stresses and changes in temperature during every take-off or landing run. Despite this, and because of the expense of aircraft tires, they are often "retreaded," a process which in the past has proved to be fallible.

The most likely cause of this crash of a Boeing Advanced 727 operated by Compania Mexicana de Aviacion was the combination of poorly maintained brakes and an incorrectly manufactured tire. It brought a tragic end to a 10-year accident-free record for the Mexican carrier.

During its take-off run at Benito Juarez airport near Mexico City the left main gear on the Mexicana Boeing Advanced 727 (Flight 940) started to bind. Unknown to the crew, the drag that this caused raised the temperature of the brakes well beyond the safe limit. When they were retracted, the brakes would have been glowing red, and in the enclosed undercarriage bay would have raised the temperature of the tires to a dangerous level.

The crew had levelled off to their cruising height of 31,000 feet (9400m) for the short 400-mile (640-km) westbound transit to Puerto Vallarta when an explosion blew out a large section of the port wing, damaging vital fuel and hydraulic lines and electrical cables. At this height this caused an explosive cabin decompression. The crew made a terse emergency report before the aircraft crashed into mountains near Maravatio, 100 miles (161km) to the north-west of Mexico City. All 159 passengers and eight crew members were killed.

Right: The Boeing 727 crashed into a wooded, mountainous area, making the job of the rescue teams even more difficult. Here rescue workers carry away the body of one of the 167 victims.

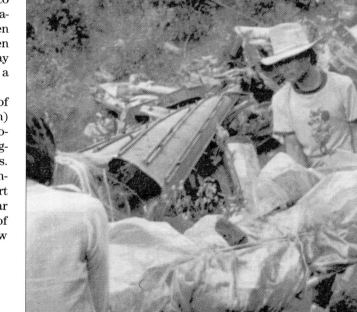

OFF SUMBURGH, SHETLAND ISLES

NOVEMBER 6, 1986

Right: British aviation minister Michael Spicer inspects pieces of the crashed Chinook helicopter that were recovered from the sea off Sumburgh.

During the 1980s British International Helicopters operated regular services under contract with the various oil companies to oil rigs and drilling platforms in the North Sea for the benefit of oil company personnel. Both Chinook and Sikorsky helicopters regularly made the journey in poor weather conditions – four accidents, two of them fatal, were recorded between 1986 and 1990. The first was the worst ever commercial helicopter accident.

The Chinook helicopter took off at approximately 1115 hours on November 6, 1986, carrying 42 workers back to Sumburgh airport near Lerwick at the end of their three-week stint on a rig in the Brent oil field.

Three miles out to sea from the airport, in strong winds and rain, the rear set of rotors on the twin rotor-craft struck the forward blades. The rear blades, and the transmission driving them, then broke away and the helicopter fell from an altitude of about 500 feet (150m) into the freezing waters of the North Sea. In all, 45 people on board died of the trauma they suffered as a result. The captain and a single passenger were plucked from the sea by a helicopter that arrived on the scene only shortly after the crash.

When wreckage recovered from the sea was analysed, it became clear that one of the main gears driving the rotor head had cracked through fatigue, possibly exacerbated by the corrosion associated with salt water operations.

OKECIE AIRPORT, POLAND

MAY 9, 1987

Even the failure of the smallest component in a commercial jetliner can spell disaster. In this tragedy, a worn ball-bearing began a series of events that led to the death of 188 people.

Filled almost to capacity, an Ilyushin IL-62 jetliner of Polskie Linie Lotnieze (LOT Polish Airlines) took off on May 9, 1987, from Okecie Airport near Warsaw on a transatlantic service to New York City.

Many of those on board were on their way to see relatives. As the aircraft climbed to its cruising altitude, at 31,000 feet (9400m), the port inner engine rapidly disintegrated, wrecking the port outer engine. Parts of both engines smashed into the passenger cabin, as well as damaging the fin and elevator. The pilot regained control, but because of the damage to the electrical system, there was no indication of the fire that had started in the hold.

Although the pilot managed to guide the stricken aircraft back to Okecie for a landing approach, the fire damage in the rear of the aircraft caused a total loss of control. The aircraft cut a wide swathe through a forest as it crashed 3 miles (5km) short of the runway, with the loss of all those on board.

Below: A fireman searching for remains of the Ilyushin airliner that crashed into a forest near Warsaw killing all those on board.

SIOUX CITY AIRPORT, IOWA, USA

JULY 19, 1989

Skilled piloting can do much to save a stricken aircraft. When the United Airlines McDonnell Douglas DC-10 crash-landed on July 19, 1989, it was only through an incredible feat of piloting that 184 of the 296 people on board the aircraft escaped with their lives.

At a height of 37,000 feet (11,277m), approximately halfway through a 930-mile (1500-km) domestic service between Denver, Colorado, and Chicago, Illinois, a loud explosion was heard from the rear of the DC-10. Instruments on the flight deck indicated that the No.2 engine mounted on the fin of the jetliner had failed. More worryingly, hydraulic pressure – which is essential to control this type of aircraft – was registering zero.

When the back-up hydraulic system also failed, the flight crew were forced to face the fact that they had a virtually uncontrollable aircraft. The only means of control available to them was to vary the thrust to the other two, wing-mounted, engines. This takes great skill and allows little room for error. Behind the tense atmosphere on the flight deck, the passengers were instructed to prepare for a crash landing.

The aircraft was closest to Sioux City Airport, where emergency services were put on full alert and all air traffic cleared from the vicinity. The aircraft pitched and rolled toward Runway 22 as the pilots fought to keep the wings level. Just 100 feet (30m) above the ground, the starboard wing dropped and struck the ground. Careering off the runway the aircraft flipped over on its back and broke up into three pieces. It then burst into flames.

Arriving on the scene within seconds, the airport firecrews battled to free passengers hanging in their seat restraints inside, but could not prevent many from being overcome by the fumes. In all, 111 passengers and a stewardess died.

After an exhaustive investigation, it was revealed that a forged titanium alloy rotor disc had shattered. This was due to a fault in the casting process that had taken place more than 18 years previously.

Above: A United Airlines McDonnell Douglas DC-10 similar to the aircraft that crash-landed at Sioux City Airport.

SUPHAN BURI, THAILAND

MAY 26, 1991

The only accident recorded to mark the otherwise exemplary record of the Australian Lauda-Air airline – former racing driver Nicki Lauda's airline – also involved a Boeing 767, which has otherwise proved to be one of the safest commercial airliners on the market.

Quite why the thrust reverser on the port engine of the Boeing 767 deployed, as the aircraft climbed under full power through 25,000 feet (7500m), has never been established. What is clear is the catastrophic effect it had. Just 16 minutes after take-off from Bangkok airport, the airliner entered a steep dive and began to disintegrate, bursting into flames and plunging into the Thai jungle. There were no survivors among the 213 passengers and 20 crew. Wreckage was scattered over a wide area, and rescue teams found their job hampered by the density of the surrounding jungle.

A further obstacle to accurate analysis of the fatal accident was the obliteration of the digital flight data recorder – the "black box". Black boxes can sometimes hold the key to the cause of a crash; but in this case it was the cockpit voice recorder that provided the clue. When the tape from the Boeing 767 was played back, the first officer was heard to say "reverser's deployed."

Working on this vital piece of evidence, investigators discovered that the most likely cause of the accident was electrical interference. The source of this is unclear, and very difficult to substantiate. It did, however, cause the thrust management to reverse the engine in flight. Reversers are only ever used to brake the aircraft on the ground run, or more obviously to reverse from a loading ramp.

As a result of this accident Boeing were forced to retrofit nearly 2000 of their jetliners with a modified thrust reversing system.

Left: Rescue workers and investigators survey some of the wreckage of the Boeing 767 that exploded and crashed in the Thai jungle.

AMSTERDAM, HOLLAND
OCTOBER 4, 1992

Right: The scene
in the
Bijlmermeer
district of
Amsterdam
shortly after the
Boeing freighter
aircraft crashed
into an apartment
house, partly
demolishing it
and setting it on
fire.

Residents in the buildings adjacent to Schipol airport, serving the Dutch port of Amsterdam, have long been campaigners against the noise and smoke pollution that is for them a daily experience. In October of 1992 an accident occurred that had an even more devastating impact on their lives.

Fully-loaded, the freighter variant of Boeing's 747 can carry some 200,000 lb (90,720kg) of cargo over 5000 miles (8045km). Design tolerances include substantial safety margins to ensure that the airframe does not become overstressed. Tragically, though, it seems that the same rigorous procedures were not applied to the testing of the connecting pins securing engines and pylons on the aircraft.

El-Al Flight 1862 was loaded almost to capacity for its return flight from Amsterdam to Ben Gurion airport in Tel Aviv. As the freighter left the runway at just after 1930 hours on the evening of October 4, 1992, a damaged pin securing the No. 3 engine and pylon sheared off, causing the engine to break away from the wing pylon. At the same time the No.4 pylon and engine were also torn off, together with part of the leading edge of the wing.

The aircraft, which was already heavily loaded, struggled to gain altitude with a substantial reduction in available power. The loss of the engine also damaged control surfaces in the wing, making the aircraft almost impossible to control. Only minutes after take-off the giant freighter smashed into the the center section of a multi-story apartment building in the Bijlmermeer district of Amsterdam.

The aircraft exploded on impact, completely destroying a large section of the building and severely damaging the surrounding structure. All four crew members and 47 of those in the apartments died in the tragedy. Hundreds more were injured.

In the investigation following the accident it transpired that the inboard midspar connecting pin that secured the No. 3 engine and pylon had corroded quite seriously, threatening the safety of the aircraft.

LONG ISLAND, NEW YORK, USA

JULY 17, 1996

Above: A TWA Boeing 747 airliner taking off.

Right: A wing section of the crashed 747 floating in the water on the south side of Long Island.

I t took nearly 15 months to piece together the Trans World Airlines (TWA) Boeing 747 that exploded in a fireball minutes after taking off from John F. Kennedy airport in New York. The investigation by the US National Transport Safety Board was the most extensive and thorough in their history, costing in excess of $50 million, but no amount of money could ever bring back the 230 people who died on that July evening.

Eighteen months after the tragedy there remained considerable uncertainty over the cause of the accident. Early indications suggested that the giant airliner had been blown out of the sky by a bomb, or a ground-to-air missile, but as the investigation progressed this theory, for which clear evidence was lacking, receded.

Another theory, with serious ramifications for the entire Boeing 747 fleet of more than 1000 aircraft, focused on the possibility that fuel vapor in the center fuel tank (located beneath the passenger floor between the wings) ignited after it became overheated. If this was indeed what had happpened, it meant that the tragedy could be repeated.

TWA Flight 800, on a scheduled service from Paris, was delayed at JFK airport for nearly three hours by mechanical problems. The center tank was virtually empty for the transatlantic flight – most of the fuel had been pumped into the wing tanks. In the sweltering July temperatures, fuel vapor would have built up above the liquid jet fuel to a temperature up to 100°F, the temperature at which the volatile fuel will ignite with the merest spark.

The aircraft finally took off and began to climb to cruising height as it flew east over Long Island. Weather conditions were near perfect. Passengers were just settling down for the long flight when, as the aircraft ascended through 13,700 feet (4100m), a huge explosion blew away a large part of the fuselage below the leading edge of the wings. The stricken 747 plunged 5000 feet (1520m) before a second explosion in the same area sealed its fate. The aircraft disintegrated, and less than 15 minutes after they had left New York, the 230 people on board were dead.

US Coast Guard, naval, and fishing vessels rushed to the scene, and for days plied the North Atlantic off Long Island recovering the shattered remains of the aircraft. Wreckage sank into the deep offshore waters over an area of six miles (9.6km). It took until May 1997 to recover most of it.

National Transport Safety Board (NTSB) investigators were in no doubt that it was the explosion of the fuel air mixture that caused the disaster. What remained unclear was what actually triggered the explosion in the first place.

On earlier models of the 747 – the aircraft involved was nearly 25 years old – thick bundles of electrical wires run aft from the flight deck. They are thickly armored with aluminum cloth and Kevlar and investigators found no evidence that they were split or worn. A possible answer may have been that faulty wiring in the proximity of the wing fuel tanks triggered a flame, which then entered the center fuel tank via a vent hole.

However, a theory that most senior NTSB officials supported was that jet fuel sloshing around in the center tank caused a build-up in static electricity, which then ignited the overheated fuel vapor. Like many air disasters, the search for an answer may drag on for years, but if this last theory did prove to be true, it would place many thousands of aircraft besides the Boeing 747 at risk.

Right: *A section of the fuselage is lifted from the naval salvage ship USS* Grapple *to a utility craft that will take it ashore for investigation.*

INDEX